$\mathcal{M}$ARY

Who She Is *and*
Why She Matters

By Robert Stackpole, STD

Director, John Paul II Institute of Divine Mercy

MARIAN PRESS
STOCKBRIDGE · MA 01263

2016

Available from:
Marian Helpers Center
Stockbridge, MA 01263
1-800-462-7426
marian.org
ShopMercy.org

Library of Congress Control Number: 2016916411
ISBN: 978-1-59614-380-7

Imprimi Potest:
Very Rev. Kazimierz Chwalek, MIC, Provincial Superior
The Blessed Virgin Mary, Mother of Mercy Province
Congregation of Marian Fathers of the Immaculate Conception
September 8, 2016
Feast of the Nativity of Mary

Printed in the United States of America

Table of Contents

FOREWORD

I want you to take the time to read this book, not just because I'm a member of a religious Congregation and think everyone should care about Mary as much as we do, or because I'm the publisher of Marian Press.

No. I want you to read this book because you can't love what you don't know — and the Blessed Virgin Mary is worth knowing and loving.

Why? Because she loves you more than anyone except God ever can and ever will. Only God loves more than the Blessed Virgin Mary, and that's because God is love. He is the reason that the Blessed Virgin Mary can love so much. God is the reason that Mary is the Immaculate Conception, the Spouse of the Holy Spirit, the Mother of God.

Dr. Robert Stackpole, a fine writer and theologian, and a long-time collaborator with my Congregation, the Marian Fathers of the Immaculate Conception, explains all that in easy-to-understand detail in this book. He's put together an accessible introduction to the basic truths about Our Lady that the Catholic Church teaches and that my Congregation shares through our pamphlets, prayercards, and books like the one you hold in your hand. He'll also share with you some of the great apparitions of Our Lady, times when she visited earth from Heaven with words of comfort, encouragement, or exhortation, with prophetic warnings and powerful devotions to meet the rising tide of trouble in the world.

Please read this book carefully, taking your time and praying over anything that really jumps out at you as you go. Maybe even highlight certain passages that seem especially profound or that you want to come back to later. Our Lady is the model

Christian — we have everything to learn from her, and we owe her everything, because Jesus comes to us through her.

Learn about Our Lady so that you might love her better. She loves you more than words can say.

May God bless you and may Our Lady always intercede for you.

In Mary Immaculate,

Fr. Chris Alar, MIC
"Father Joseph, MIC"
Director, Association of Marian Helpers
September 8, 2016
Feast of the Nativity of Mary in the extraordinary
Jubilee Year of Mercy

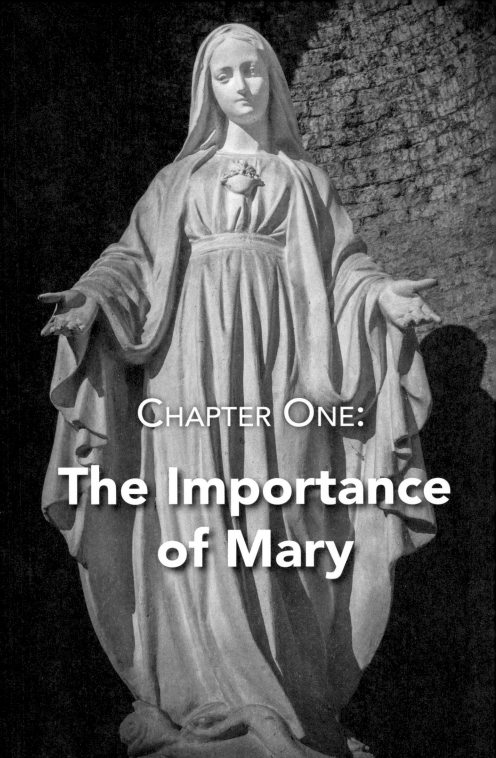

CHAPTER ONE:

The Importance of Mary

Why is the Blessed Virgin Mary so important in the Catholic faith? Protestant Christians ask this question of Catholics all the time. But do we Catholics really know how to answer it?

Many Catholics are stumped when they hear Evangelical Protestants say things like this:

> Catholics make Mary too important. You even worship Mary, which the First Commandment clearly forbids, for we must not worship anyone other than God. According to the Bible, salvation is found in Jesus Christ alone.

This book is designed to help Catholics answer such objections, and to more deeply appreciate the special role that God gave to Mary in His plan of salvation through Jesus Christ. You will also find guidance to help you welcome Mary into your life, for, as we shall see, she is far more than just a set of doctrines to believe in: She is also the model of all faithful Christian discipleship, and our true spiritual mother in Heaven.

As for "worshipping" Mary as a god or as God, of course Catholics are not allowed to do such a thing. To "worship" someone or something implies that one recognizes in the object of worship the source of all worth and goodness. But the Catholic Church teaches that Mary is certainly not the source of all worth and goodness in the universe; she is just a creature, a human being who freely surrendered herself to be a channel and vessel of God's grace. We call her "Holy Mary" in somewhat the same way that all Christians speak of the "Holy Bible," because the Bible, too, is a vessel, a channel of God's grace to us. As St. Ambrose (340-397) once wrote: "Mary is the Temple of God, not the God of the Temple."

In technical, theological language, we say that we offer "worship" (in Latin, *latria*) to God alone; what we offer to any created excellence fashioned by God is either merely "veneration" or "honor" (in Latin, *dulia*) such as the honor we give to the saints, or "highest honor" (*hyperdulia*) the veneration Catholics offer to Mary. Honoring Mary and the saints no more distracts us from the true worship of God than delighting in and praising an artist's best work distracts us from proper appreciation of the artist himself. Clearly, the honor given to the excellence of the artwork passes on and glorifies the artist, and the artist's best work gives us all the more reason to appreciate and praise him. In a similar way, God is the artist of souls, by the Holy Spirit. As we shall see in the pages that follow, He has fashioned no greater masterpiece in all of creation than the Mother of the Son of God, Mary of Nazareth.

This means that when Catholics gaze on Mary, we always see, shining in and through her, the light of her Son; she is the pure reflection of His merciful and compassionate Heart. Here, then, is the first reason why the Blessed Virgin Mary is so important to Catholics: because she is like a window into Heaven, a true icon for us of the merciful love of God, who created and sanctified her. Archbishop Fulton Sheen summed it up best in his book *The World's First Love*:

> God, who made the sun, also made the moon. The moon does not take away from the brilliance of the sun. The moon would only be a burnt-out cinder floating in the immensity of space were it not for the sun. All its light is reflected from the sun. The Blessed Mother reflects her Divine Son: without Him she is nothing. With Him she is the Mother of Men. On dark nights we are grateful for the moon; when we see it shining, we know there must be a sun. So in this dark night of the world, when men turn their backs on Him Who is the Light of the World, we look to Mary to guide their feet while we await the sunrise.[1]

Devotion to Mary and the Worship of Idols

Nevertheless, some of our Evangelical brothers and sisters will object:

> But you Catholics *do* worship Mary and the saints: You make images and statues of them and bow down

and pray to them, and you carry these images and statues in religious processions. All of this violates the Ten Commandments, which strictly forbid the people of God from making images of things in Heaven, and from the worship of idols.

Theologian Mark Miravalle, in his book *Introduction to Mary*, explains that these actions by Catholics do not imply that we worship her, or even that we worship the statues and images of her that we use in religious devotion:

> A painting or a statue of the Mother of Jesus serves the same purpose as a family photo on an office desk, or a statue of a public hero or statesman erected in a town square. The image serves as a reminder of the person the image represents, and thereby possesses a symbolic or representational value ...
>
> As a father gazes upon the photograph of his family on his desk at work and feels the warming of his heart at the thought of his wife and children, so too, an image of Jesus' Mother can evoke similar feelings of filial love and devotion to her. Yet, as is true of the family photo and the public memorial statue, the Marian statue or image possesses no intrinsic power nor personhood; it only conveys an image of a Spiritual Mother most deserving of frequent remembrance and love.[2]

Besides, it is clear from Scripture that not all making and devout use of religious images amounts to "the worship of idols." For example, in the Old Testament, the Lord God commanded the making of two cherubim of gold to be set over the Mercy Seat on the Ark of the Covenant (see Ex 25:18-20). When God gave to Kings David and Solomon the divine plan for the building of the Great Temple in Jerusalem, it was to be adorned with carved wooden cherubim (see 1 Kgs 6:23-26; 1 Chr 28:18-19). The prophet Ezekiel also describes carved cherubim in the ideal Temple that was shown to him in a vision (see Ez 4:17-18). Moses was actually commanded to make a bronze serpent and set it on a pole, so that any Israelite who looked upon it might be healed (see Num 21:8-9). This shows that religious images can be used, not only for decoration, but even as aids to devotion and faith. Of course, when the Israelites began to worship the bronze serpent itself as a snake-god, King Hezekiah rightly had it destroyed (see 2 Kgs 18:4). But it is clear from the Bible that not all religious use of images and statues amounts to idolatry.

Even "bowing down" to them or kneeling to pray before them is not necessarily an act of worship. Bowing and kneeling can mean different things in different cultures. For example, in Japan, people bow to each other simply to show mutual respect and honor. Kneeling can be an act of humility, love, and supplication as we ask for the prayers of the particular angel or saint depicted in an image or statue. The intention is simply that the veneration or supplication we offer passes on to the person that the image represents. Catholics certainly do not intend to ask the paint on a canvas or the plaster or wood in a statue to hear their prayers!

Speaking of the Ten Commandments, we might well ask: Did Jesus keep them? All Christians surely believe that Jesus was without sin, the spotless Lamb of God, so He must have kept all of God's commandments perfectly. But that means that He also kept the commandment to "honor your father and your mother" perfectly. As Christians, we are to be disciples of Jesus Christ, and to follow His perfect example of love for God and for one another. It follows that if Jesus honored His mother and father (that is, the Blessed Virgin Mary and St. Joseph), then, as His followers, we should honor them, too. As St. Maximilian Kolbe once said, "Never be afraid of loving the Blessed Virgin too much. You can never love her more than Jesus did."

Mary and Salvation Through Christ Alone

Many of our Evangelical brothers and sisters claim that we should trust in Jesus Christ, and in Him "alone," for our salvation — not in Mary and the saints. But from a Catholic perspective, this runs into one big problem: The Bible clearly tells us that *Jesus is never alone!* Yes, our trust is ultimately in Him, and He is "pre-eminent in all things" (Col 1:18), but He is never solitary: He is King of a Kingdom, the unifying center and source of the whole Communion of Saints, the Head of a Body in which we are all members. To be fully united with Him is to be "in Christ," which includes being "in" His Body, the Church (see 1 Cor 12:12-27). The Book of Hebrews tells us that when you come to Jesus, "You have come to Mount Zion and to the city of the living God, the heavenly Jerusalem, and to innumerable angels in festal gathering, and to the assembly of the first-born who are enrolled in heaven, and to a judge who is God of all, and to the spirits of just men made perfect, and to Jesus, the mediator of a new covenant ..." (Heb 12:22-24). In other words, when we come to Jesus, we become part of a whole community of faith that embraces both Heaven and earth, *and His grace flows to us through this community of faith, precisely because it is His Body.*

In fact, the Bible says that whenever we repent of our sins and turn to Christ, we are re-established as members of the very "household of God" (1 Tim 3:15); in other words, we are accepted back into the family of the Son of God Himself, just as the Prodigal Son was welcomed home in Jesus' parable (see Lk 15:11-32). And just as in any loving family on earth, the family of Christ is full of mutual help and support. Catholic theologian Scott Hahn explains this beautiful truth — and what it implies about our relationship with Mary — in his book *Hail, Holy Queen*:

> God's covenant family is perfect, lacking nothing. The Church looks to God as Father, Jesus as Brother, and to heaven as home. What is missing then?
>
> In truth, nothing. Every family needs a mother; only Christ could choose His own, and He chose providentially for His entire covenant family. Now everything He has He shares with us. His divine life is ours [e.g., II Pet 1:4]; His home is our home [Jn 14:1-4]; His father is our Father [Mt 6:9]; His brothers are our brothers [Mk 3:35], and His mother is our mother, too [Jn 19:25-27].

For a family is incomplete without a loving mother. The breakaway Christian churches that diminish Mary's role inevitably end up feeling like a bachelor's apartment: masculine to a fault; orderly but not homey; functional and productive — but with little sense of beauty and poetry.

Yet all the Scriptures … all creation, and our deepest human needs tell us that no family should be that way — and certainly not the covenant family of God. The apostles knew this, and that's why they were gathered with Mary in Jerusalem at Pentecost. The early generations of Christians knew this, and that's why they painted her image in their catacombs and dedicated their churches to her.[3]

The Game Plan of This Book

An ever-deepening understanding of the full truth about Mary as our spiritual mother in the family of God has gradually unfolded in the life of the Church over many centuries. Saints, popes, and church councils, under the guidance of the Holy Spirit, have pondered ever more deeply the words of Scripture about Mary's role in God's plan. Step by step, the early Christians came to appreciate the revealed truth about Our Lady. In this book on Mary, therefore, we will walk through these truths one at a time in roughly the same order that the Church herself came to appreciate and fully articulate them down through history. First, we will ponder themes that were especially close to the hearts of the earliest Christians and the ancient Fathers of the Church: namely, Mary as the New Eve and the Ever-Virgin Mother of God. Then we will consider truths about Mary that were articulated for the first time in the Middle Ages (although as we shall see, the first seeds of these doctrines were planted in the soil of the Church's life by the Holy Spirit from the beginning): the doctrines that Mary was filled with divine grace from the very first moment of her existence, and assumed body and soul into Heaven at her life's end. Finally we will show that she reigns now with her Son as Queen of Heaven and our spiritual Mother of Mercy, and that her Immaculate Heart is truly the heart of the Church.

Some of these revealed truths about Mary have been solemnly and infallibly defined by the Church's Magisterium, namely that we are to call Mary Mother of God and Ever Virgin, that she was conceived without sin and assumed body and soul into Heaven at her life's end. We call these the four Marian "dogmas." Other Catholic doctrines about Mary are so solidly attested in Scripture (at least implicitly) as well as in Sacred Tradition, especially in the writings of many great saints and popes, that we can hold them as true beyond any reasonable doubt, even though they have never been solemnly defined: for example, Mary as the New Eve, Queen of Heaven, and Mother of Mercy. Some doctrines about Mary, and their roots in Scripture and Tradition, are still being discerned and debated today by theologians and the Magisterium, such as the precise meaning of Mary's titles of "Co-Redemptrix" and "Mediatrix of All Graces."

Although this book is written primarily for Catholics, we hope that it will stimulate friendly discussion with our Evangelical brothers and sisters as well, and lead to greater mutual understanding of the role that Mary plays in God's plan.

In the chapters that follow, we will walk through each of these wonderful, divinely revealed truths about the Blessed Virgin, and invite the reader to a deeper devotion to Mary as the one whose sole task, both on earth and in Heaven, is to bring us ever closer to the Merciful Heart of Jesus, her Son.

PRAYER

> O Blessed Virgin Mary, I humbly beseech thee …
> through thy pure heart, to take full possession of my
> heart. Give it completely to thy divine Son, and beg
> Him to banish from it all sin and to establish in it forever
> the perfect reign of His divine love (St. John Eudes).

QUESTIONS FOR DISCUSSION

1. What is the difference between forbidden "worship" of Mary and the "veneration" of Mary encouraged by the Church?

2. What difference does it make to the Church as the family of God to have a loving mother?

3. Does having a personal relationship with Mary *necessarily* compete with, or distract us from, our personal relationship with Jesus Christ as Lord and Savior? Can some people go too far and put Mary at the center of their lives *instead of Jesus*?

SUGGESTIONS FOR FURTHER READING

- *Catechism of the Catholic Church*, entry 971

- The section from Fr. Donald Calloway, MIC's book *Under the Mantle* (Marian Press, 2013) entitled "Who Do You Say that I Am?" pp. 37-47, which gives Fr. Don's personal witness about the importance of Mary to his own conversion, and to the fullness of life in Christ

CHAPTER TWO

Mary,
the New Eve

In North America, when children are playing games together and want a second opportunity to score a goal or hit a home run, they ask their companions for a "do-over," a second chance.

The first thing that the early Church taught about Mary was that she was an integral part of the do-over that God gave to the world through Jesus Christ. The New Testament tells us that Jesus is the "Second Adam" (for instance, Rom 5:12-21): in other words, the beginning of a "do-over" for the whole fallen race of Adam. As Adam was the head of fallen humanity, so Jesus becomes the Head of a new, redeemed, and sanctified humanity.

At the same time, the Blessed Virgin Mary is clearly shown in Scripture to be the Second Eve. Remember that in the Book of Genesis, the first Eve, Mother of All the Living, ushered in the age of sin by succumbing to the temptation of a fallen angel, the serpent (the devil in disguise!) in the Garden of Eden. Mary is the New Eve because she *reversed* Eve's sin by her obedience to a *good* angel, the angel Gabriel, at the Annunciation in Nazareth (see Lk 1:26-28).

The Faith of the Early Christians

That Mary is rightly seen as the New Eve in God's plan of salvation for the human race was the common teaching of the earliest "Fathers" of the Church (that is, the greatest writers of the early centuries of Christianity). In the mid-second century, for example, only about 100 years after the death and resurrection of Jesus, St. Justin Martyr tells us in his *Dialogue with Tryphon* (section 100):

> Eve, a virgin and undefiled, conceived the word of the serpent, and bore disobedience and death. But the Virgin Mary received faith and joy when the angel Gabriel announced to her the glad tidings that the Spirit of the Lord would come upon her, and the power of the Most High would overshadow her, for which reason the Holy One being born of her is the Son of God. And she replied: "Be it done unto me according to thy word."

In the same century, we find a similar teaching in the works of Tertullian of Carthage in North Africa (*De Carn. Christ.* 17):

> What by that [female] sex had gone into perdition, by that same sex might be brought back to salvation. Eve had believed the serpent; Mary believed Gabriel; the fault which the one committed by believing, the other by believing has blotted out.

Again, we find a similar teaching echoed in the writings of the great second-century Church Father St. Irenaeus of Lyons, in his main work *Against Heresies* (III. 22. 34). It should be noted that St. Irenaeus had learned the Catholic faith earlier in the second century from St. Polycarp, bishop of Smyrna in Asia Minor, who in turn had learned the faith from St. John the Apostle himself. Saint Irenaeus wrote:

> Just as Eve, wife of Adam, yet still a virgin, became by her disobedience the cause of death for herself and the whole human race, so Mary, too, espoused yet a Virgin, became by her obedience the cause of salvation for herself and the whole human race ... And so it was that the knot of Eve's disobedience was loosed by Mary's obedience. For what the virgin bound fast by her refusal to believe, this the Virgin Mary unbound by her belief.

In other words, according to St. Irenaeus, the human race was all tied up in knots as a result of Eve's fall from grace, but those knots were untangled by the Blessed Virgin. (Perhaps now we can see why Pope Francis has encouraged Catholics to turn to "Mary, Undoer of Knots" in the troubled times in which we live today!) Again in the same work, St. Irenaeus wrote (v.19):

> As Eve by the speech of an angel was seduced so as to flee God, transgressing His word, so also Mary received the good tidings by means of the angel's speech, so as to bear God within her, being obedient to His word. And, though one had disobeyed God, yet the other was drawn to obey God; that of the Virgin

Eve, the Virgin Mary might become the advocate. And as by a virgin the human race had been bound by death, by a virgin it is saved, the balance being preserved, a virgin's disobedience by a virgin's obedience.

In short, according to St. Irenaeus, Mary's obedience to God began the liberation of humanity from the bondage to sin and death that Eve's disobedience to God had initially set in motion.

This doctrine of Mary as the New Eve in God's plan of salvation also can be found in numerous places in the writings of the later Church Fathers. In the fourth century, for example, St. Epiphanius of Cyprus wrote: "Eve became a cause of death to men ... and Mary a cause of life" (*Haer.* 78.18); St. Jerome's slogan was "Death by Eve, life by Mary" (*Ep. Ad Eustoch.* 22.21); St. Peter Chrysologus (d. 450 A.D.) echoes the same teaching: "Woman now is truly made through grace Mother of the living, who had been by nature mother of the dying."

These reflections by the early Church Fathers provide the beginning of an answer to those who claim that Catholicism treats women as second-class citizens in the Church. "If in the Bible Eve is blamed for the fall of man long ago, and women cannot be priests today," it is said, "then women are hardly seen as equal to men in the eyes of the Catholic Church." On the contrary, women are in some respects even *greater* than men in the eyes of the Church, for Mary reversed Eve's sin in the Garden by her obedience to the angel Gabriel, and of all the creatures who have ever lived, the greatest is the New Eve, the mother of the divine Savior, who alone among created human beings was called by an angel "full of grace" (Lk 1:28). As we shall see later in this book (Chapter Seven), Mary reigns now with her Son as Queen of His Kingdom, above all the angels and saints in Heaven, and above all the bishops and priests on earth.

Notice also that while the early Church Fathers were teaching that Mary is the New Eve, none of them thought that this belief in any way distracted Christians from their fundamental conviction that Jesus alone is our Lord and Savior. On the contrary, they called Mary the New Eve precisely because she cooperated in a unique way with the saving work of the Son of God.

The New Eve and the Annunciation

Do we appreciate what tremendous things Mary did for the world at the Annunciation, when she acted as the New Eve in God's plan and thereby ushered in the dawn of salvation?

First of all, she gave us the perfect example of Christian discipleship. After all, what does it mean to be a disciple of Jesus Christ, if not to surrender completely to our Heavenly Father's plan for our lives? Each one of us has a special vocation to serve the Kingdom of God according to a unique call — whether as married or as single people, as parents or grandparents, as workers in the business world or in private charities, as doctors or nurses, as teachers or civil servants, as clergy or religious — whatever it may be, each one of us is graced by the Holy Spirit to enable us to respond to His call. Only when we respond with total, trustful surrender, as Mary did, can we fully become His faithful disciples and truly "magnify the Lord" as she did (Lk 1:46-55). That is why the Anglican-Roman Catholic International Commission (ARCIC), in their great ecumenical Agreed Statement entitled "Mary: Grace and Hope in Christ" (2004), emphasized so strongly this aspect of her significance for all Christians:

> Mary, as the Mother of our Lord Jesus Christ, stands before us as an exemplar of faithful obedience, and her "Be it unto me according to your word" is the grace-filled response that each of us is called to make to God, both personally and communally as the Church, the Body of Christ. It is as a figure of the Church, her arms uplifted in prayer and praise, her hands open in receptivity and availability to the outpouring of the Holy Spirit, that we are one with Mary as she magnifies the Lord.[4]

Second, by saying "yes" to the angel Gabriel at the Annunciation, Mary thereby received Christ into the world "in the fullness of time" (Gal 4:4); in other words, when the time was just right for God's plan of salvation to be accomplished.

Saint Bernard of Clairvaux (1090-1153; sometimes called "the last of the Fathers of the Church") wrote the following meditation on the Annunciation story. It beautifully sums up for us the tremendous importance of what God's grace accomplished through Mary at that critical moment in the history of the human race. In a nutshell, he says that the whole universe held its breath, waiting to see what Mary would say in response to the angel:

> You [Mary] have heard that you will conceive and bear a son. You have heard that it will be by the Holy Spirit and not by a man. The angel is waiting for your reply. It is time for him to return to the One who sent him.
>
> We too are waiting for this merciful word, my Lady, we who are miserably weighed down under a sentence of condemnation. The price of our salvation is being offered to you. If you consent we shall immediately be set free. We have all been made in the eternal Word of God, and look, we are dying. In your brief reply we shall be restored and brought back to life. Doleful Adam and his unhappy offspring, exiled from paradise, implore you, kind Virgin, to give this answer. David asks it. Abraham asks it. All the other holy patriarchs, your very own fathers, beg it of you, as do those now dwelling in the region of the shadow of death. For it the whole world is waiting, bowed down at your feet. And rightly, too, because on your answer depends the comfort of the afflicted, the deliverance of the damned, the salvation of the sons of Adam, your whole race. Give your answer quickly, my Virgin. My Lady, say this word which earth and hell and heaven itself are waiting for. The very King and Lord of all, He who has so desired your beauty, is eager for your answer and assent, by which he proposes to save the world. Him whom you pleased by your silence, you will now please even more by your word ... Blessed Virgin, open your heart to faith, your lips to consent, and your womb to your Creator. Behold the long-desired of all

nations is standing at the door and is knocking. Oh, what if He should pass by because of your delay, and sorrowing, you should again have to seek Him whom your soul loves? Get up, run, open! Get up by faith, run by prayer, open by consent!

"Behold," she says, "I am the handmaiden of the Lord. Let it be done to me according to your word."[5]

Later in the Gospel story, at the Wedding Feast at Cana, Jesus addresses His mother in a way that alludes to her role as the New Eve in God's plan of salvation. When Mary brought to His attention the needs of the married couple, saying, "They have no wine," Jesus responded, "O woman, what have you to do with me? My hour has not yet come" (Jn 2:3-4). In the English translation, it sounds like a rebuke — and a disrespectful one at that! (Sons do not ordinarily refer to their own mothers as "woman"!) However, it is hardly likely that Jesus Christ would be rude to His own mother, and given that He subsequently granted her request about the wine, He can hardly have meant His response to her as a rebuke.

As a matter of fact, understood in the context of the time, the words Jesus spoke are actually full of profound meaning. The phrase is a Hebrew idiom, which has been translated by the Gospel writer into Greek. Rendered literally, it is: "What to me and to you?" In other words, "What is the significance of your request for us both?" Jesus is saying to her, in effect: "Do you realize what you are asking of Me? By granting your request, I will be setting in motion a series of events that will inevitably bring about the 'hour' of My Passion." Thus, just as Eve initiated the *fall* of the human race by taking forbidden fruit from a tree, so Mary, the New Eve, by her intercession, initiated the *salvation* of the human race through the saving work of Christ, a work that can be completed only by the "hour" of His Passion on the tree of the Cross.

The mystery of this Gospel passage, however, goes deeper still. In biblical times, a man might address a female with respect as "woman" (the equivalent of "madam"), and Jesus addresses several women in this fashion in St. John's Gospel (see Jn 4:21,

8:10, and 20:15), but nowhere in the ancient world do we have anyone on record addressing his own mother with such a title. This is an indication that our Lord was pointing to something important by using this form of address for Mary — and its significance is not hard to see. "Woman" is the name that Adam gave to Eve in Genesis 2:23. Moreover, in the first prophecy of the Messiah in the whole Bible, Genesis 3:15, we are promised that one day the seed of "the woman" will crush the evil serpent's head (that is, her child will destroy the power of the devil). In short, here at the Wedding Feast at Cana, Jesus, the New Adam, addresses Mary as the "woman" of Genesis, the New Eve in God's plan.

Though the first Eve failed to trust and obey God in the Garden of Eden, eating the fruit from the forbidden tree instead, the New Eve surrendered her Heart completely to God at the Annunciation. This tremendous act of total, trustful surrender then deepened at the Wedding Feast at Cana and, as we shall see, reached its zenith beneath the Cross on Calvary. In fact, it is on Calvary, from the Cross, the tree of salvation, that Jesus will once again call His mother "woman" (see Jn 19:25-27): the woman of Genesis 3:15, the New Eve in God's plan of salvation for the whole human race.

PRAYER

> Lord Jesus Christ, help me to follow the example of Mary, always ready to do Your will. At the message of an Angel, she welcomed You, God's Son, and filled with the light of Your Spirit, she became Your temple. Through her prayers for me, take away my weakness, and make the offering of my life with You in the Holy Sacrifice of the Mass pleasing to You and to the Father. May I rejoice in the gift of Your grace and be united with You and Mary in glory. Amen.
>
> (Fr. Lawrence Lovasik, SVD)

QUESTIONS FOR DISCUSSION

1. What is the Biblical parallel between the story of Eve and the serpent in the Garden of Eden, and the story of Mary and the angel Gabriel in the village of Nazareth?

2. Why do you think it can be helpful to us today to read the consensus reflections of the great early Christian writers, the Fathers of the Church, on the message of Scripture?

3. Has God ever asked you to say "yes" to His plan for you and/or your family in some surprising and significant way?

SUGGESTIONS FOR FURTHER READING

- Luke 1:26-38

- Father Calloway's description of how God graciously "courted" Mary, His "feminine masterpiece," until she freely consented to be the mother of His Son, from his book *Under the Mantle*, the section entitled "Capture Her Heart," pp. 259-265

CHAPTER THREE

Mary,
Mother of God

The early Christians usually referred to Mary in their writings in one of two ways. First, they simply called her "the Virgin" (a reference to the miracle of the virginal conception of Jesus Christ in her womb, and also to Mary's lifelong virginity), and second, they called her the "Mother of God." In his book *Introduction to Mary*, Catholic theologian Mark Miravalle explains for us what this second title means:

> Mary is the Mother of Jesus; Jesus is God; therefore Mary is Mother of God. Since Jesus is truly the Son of God, and Mary is repeatedly referred to in Scripture as the "Mother of Jesus" (Mt 2:13; Jn 2:1; Acts 1:14; etc.), then Mary must be the true Mother of God made man.
>
> St. Paul also witnesses to the Divine Maternity when he states in his letter to the Galatians: "When the fullness of time had come, God sent forth his Son, born of a woman" (Gal 4:4).[6]

We need to be clear that the early Christians never claimed that Mary was the Mother of the Son of God in Heaven *before He came to earth* — that would be impossible! Mary is a creature, and a creature cannot bring into existence a divine Person in Heaven. After all, the divine Son of God exists eternally, whereas Mary only came into existence at her own conception and birth in the first century B.C. By calling her the "Mother of God," the early Christians simply meant to say that she was the Mother of the divine Son of God *in His human form* — the Mother of God *Incarnate* ("*incarnate*" comes from the Latin "*incarnatus*," which means "in the flesh").

Two key Scripture passages that the early Fathers frequently cited in defense of this title for Mary were Isaiah 7:14 and Luke 1:43. Isaiah's prophetic promises of the coming of Christ include this familiar one: "Behold, a young woman [or virgin] shall conceive and bear a son, and shall call his name Immanuel" (meaning "God with us"). In other words, the Messiah was to be born of a woman, and yet He would be in truth God dwelling in our midst. Then in Luke 1:43, when St. Elizabeth heard the greeting of her kinswoman, Mary, she exclaimed with joy: "And why is this granted to me, that the mother of my Lord should come to me?" Saint Luke evidently intends his Jewish-Christian readers to catch the reference here in Elizabeth's words to the story of King David bringing the Ark of the Covenant up to Jerusalem, when David exclaimed with fear and joy: "How can the Ark of the Lord come to me?" (2 Sam 6:9ff). In short, St. Elizabeth is referring to Mary as a new "Ark" of the Lord; her body is the Ark, and within her womb she carries the Lord Himself. Mary is therefore the Mother of our divine Lord, the Mother of "God with us" in human form.

Again, Miravalle explains:

> What precisely does Mary give to Jesus in her act of motherhood? First of all, Mary did not give Jesus his divine nature [that is, his divine attributes such as infinite power, knowledge, and love], nor did Mary give Jesus his divine personhood. Both of these divine aspects of Jesus Christ existed from all eternity. However, "when in the fullness of time, God sent his Son, born of a woman" (Gal 4:4), Mary gave to Jesus a human nature identical to her own.[7]

On the other hand, it would not be true to say that Mary was the mother only of Christ's human nature, because no one can give birth to something vague and abstract like "human nature." Mothers do not give birth to "human nature" or human "attributes" in the abstract, but to persons with a human nature. In other words, a real, flesh-and-blood "human nature" always has to belong to someone; it has to be "someone's" human nature that is born. In this case, the "someone" was the divine Second Person of the Blessed Trinity, the Son of God: It was the divine Son Himself, in His human nature, who was present in Mary's womb, and who was born in Bethlehem. That is why we can say that Mary was the Mother of God: because the Son of God received His human flesh from her and was born from her as a fully human being.

This is the wonder of the Incarnation: God the Father loved us so much that He sent His only Son into the world to be one of us, to share our human condition and human limitations, and to walk with us through all the joys and sorrows of a real human life. And just like us, He began His human journey in the womb of an earthly mother.

The Witness of the Early Church Fathers

Blessed John Henry Newman tells us that Christian writers in the early Church never ceased to wonder at this mystery, that the divine Son came down from Heaven and humbled Himself to be born of a virgin. While the reader may not recognize the names of all the saints and early Church Fathers that Newman mentions, the sheer number of them and the fact that they come from all over the ancient Christian world is certainly a sign that this consensus among the greatest teachers of early Christianity was a work of the Holy Spirit. Newman wrote:

> Christians were accustomed from the first to call the Blessed Virgin "the Mother of God," because they saw that it was impossible to deny her this title without denying St. John's words, "The Word" (that is, God the Son) "was made flesh." ...
>
> The title *Theotokos* [in Greek, literally, "the God-bearer"], as ascribed to the Blessed Virgin Mary begins with ecclesiastical writers of a date hardly later than that at which we read of her as the Second Eve. It first occurs in the works of Origen (185-254), but he, witnessing for Egypt and Palestine, witnesses also that it was in use before his time ...
>
> In the fourth [century, St.] Athanasius ... uses it many times with emphasis, [as does St.] Cyril of Palestine, [St.] Gregory of Nyssa and [St.] Gregory Nazianzen of Cappadocia ... The emperor Constantine, in his speech before the assembled bishops of Nicea [in 325 A.D.], uses the still more explicit title

of the "Virgin Mother of God;" which is also used by [St.] Vincent ... in the south of France, and then by [Pope] St. Leo.

So much for the term; it would be tedious to produce the passages of authors who, using or not using [the title], convey the idea. "Our God was carried in the womb of Mary," says St. Ignatius, who was martyred in A.D. 106. "The Word of God," says [St.] Hippolytus, "was carried in that Virgin frame." "The Maker of all," says Amphilochius, "is born of a Virgin"... "God dwelt in the womb," says [St.] Proclus ... "He is made in thee," says [St.] Augustine, "who made thee."[8]

In fact, the early Christians believed that this title for Mary, "Mother of God," was a summary of the whole mystery of the Incarnation. As a result, they defined it as a doctrine of the faith at the Ecumenical Council of Ephesus (431 A.D.), declaring the Blessed Virgin Mary to be the "Mother of God" (in Greek, the "*Theotokos*"). This also ratified the teachings of St. Cyril, the Patriarch of Alexandria at the time, who had written: "Emmanuel [Jesus Christ] in truth is God, and on this account the Holy Virgin is the Mother of God in as much as she gave birth to the Word of God made flesh."

Mary's Unique Intimacy With the Son of God, and Her Extraordinary Sanctity

Mary's official ecclesiastical title "Mother of God," however, is more than just a helpful way to sum up the mystery of the Incarnation. It also tells us something very important about Mary herself; it tells us of her *unique relationship with God*. Simply put: The divine Son of God on earth was her own Son. She gave life to Him in her own womb, gave birth to Him, and nourished Him from her own breast. She cared for Him in His time of weakness and littleness, and knew His tears and smiles better than anyone else ever could. Blessed John Henry Newman loved to meditate on this unique closeness of Mary with her Son and all the spiritual blessings she must have received from Him as a result:

> Now, consider that Mary loved her Divine Son with an unutterable love; and consider too she had him all to herself for thirty years. *Do we not see that as she was full of grace before she conceived him in her womb, she must have had a vast incomprehensible sanctity when she had lived close to God for thirty years?* — a sanctity of an angelical order, reflecting back the attributes of God with a fullness and exactness of which no saint upon earth, or hermit or holy virgin, can even remind us ...
>
> The Word and Wisdom of God once dwelt in her, and then, after his birth of her, was carried in her arms and seated in her lap in his first years. Thus, being as it were the human throne of him who reigns in heaven, she is called the Seat of Wisdom ...
>
> For if such close and continued intimacy with her Son created in her a sanctity inconceivably great, must not also the knowledge which she gained during those many years from his conversation of present, past, and future have been so large, and so profound, and so diversified, and so thorough, that, though she was a poor woman without human advantages, she must have excelled ... in her theological knowledge the greatest of theologians, and in her prophetic discernment the most favored of prophets.
>
> What was the grand theme of conversation between her and her Son but the nature, the attributes, the providence, and the works of Almighty God? Would not our Lord be ever glorifying the Father who sent him? Would he not unfold to her the solemn, eternal decrees, and the purposes and the will of God? ...
>
> Moses had the privilege [of speaking to God directly] only now and then, from time to time. But Mary for thirty continuous years saw and heard him, being able to ask him any question which she wished explained, and knowing that the answers she received

were from the eternal God, who neither deceives nor can be deceived ...

So it was with Mary. For thirty years she was blessed with the continual presence of her Son — nay, she had him in subjection. But the time came when that war called for him for which he had come upon the earth. Certainly he came, not simply to be the Son of Mary, but to be the Savior of Man, and therefore at length he parted from her. She knew then what it was to be the mother of a soldier. He left her side; she saw him no longer; she tried in vain to get near him [Mk 3:31-35]. He had for years lived in her embrace, and after that, at least in her dwelling — but now, in his own words, "The Son of Man had nowhere to lay his head." And then, when years had run out, she heard of his arrest, his mock trial, and his Passion.

At last she got near him — when and where? — on the way to Calvary, and when he had been lifted up on the cross. And at length she held him again in her arms; yes — when he was dead.[9]

Clearly, by reason of her unique closeness to Jesus, from Bethlehem to Calvary, the Blessed Virgin Mary must have attained a supreme beauty and sanctity of spirit, a depth of faith and love in her Heart that made her completely holy, unblemished by sin.

Of course, someone might object to Newman's meditation here by arguing that Mary's role as the Mother of Jesus does not automatically guarantee that she became completely holy through her 30 years of close contact with Him.

Some Protestant Evangelicals point out that Scripture teaches in several places that all human beings are sinners. The Bible says, "There is no one righteous, no not one" (Ps 14:1-3; 53); "all have sinned and fallen short of the glory of God" (Rom 3:23); and "through one man's offence, judgment came to all men" (Rom 5:18).

However, the Scriptures often use broad language, even hyperbole, in order to make a point. For example, when the Bible says "all have sinned" or "all we like sheep have gone astray," it obviously does not intend to include children, who have never committed any actual, personal sins (and if they die before attaining the age of reason, never will). Again, when the Bible says "as in Adam all die, even so in Christ shall all be made alive" (1 Cor 15:22), St. Paul evidently does not mean to tell us that the whole human race will be saved through Christ. According to St. Paul, some souls will be eternally lost (see Rom 2:6-8; 2 Thess 1:7-10). The passages in Scripture that speak of the universal commission of acts of sin by the human race, or the universal fallen condition of humanity, therefore, may be said to refer to the mass of mankind in general, excluding little children and special cases such as the Blessed Virgin Mary.

Another serious objection to the entire holiness of Mary is that she seems to proclaim herself a sinner when she brings the Christ Child to the Temple in Jerusalem. In accordance with Jewish Law, she offered for herself, with St. Joseph, "a pair of turtledoves or two young pigeons" — a sacrifice that the Old Testament tells us was a sacrifice for "atonement" (see Lk 2:22-24; see also Lev 12:7-8). If Mary made an atonement offering in the Temple, doesn't that mean that she knew herself to be a sinner?

Here we have to be careful to put ourselves in the mindset of the ancient Israelites. The dividing line between the understanding of sin that treats it as breaking God's moral commandments and the broader understanding of sin that included simply falling short of ritual purity was never entirely clarified in the Old Testament Law. Thus, the reason why a woman had to offer a sacrifice for sin in the Temple after child-birth, according to Leviticus 12:7, was because she was considered "unclean" due to "the flow of blood" involved in giving birth, not because of any personal sin she had committed.

Furthermore, the fact that Mary willingly offered this sacrifice no more implies that she is a sinner (or even that she had a flow of blood during the miraculous birth of her Son) than the fact that Jesus accepted a baptism for repentance at the hands of St. John the Baptist necessarily implies that He believed Himself to be a sinner. Our Lord's baptism was an expression of His identification with His people Israel in their longing for a fresh start in their relationship with God. As Jesus said to St. John the Baptist, who was reluctant to baptize Him, "Let it be so now; for thus it is fitting for us to fulfill all righteousness" (Mt 3:15).

In a similar way, Mary wanted to express her sharing in the longing of every Jewish mother, at the birth of every male child, for the coming of the Messiah. The rites they accomplished that day in the Temple included this very intention. "And when the time came for their purification according to the law of Moses, they brought him up to Jerusalem to present him to the Lord, as it is written in the law of the Lord, 'Every male that opens the womb shall be called holy to the Lord'" (Lk 2:22-23; see also Ex 13:2). Thus, she and St. Joseph presented the Child Jesus to the Lord in the Temple in thanksgiving, and as a Jewish mother, she offered a sacrifice as well for her own ritual (not moral) purification, though, strictly speaking, she did not need to do so.

Then what about the woman in the Gospels who cried out to Jesus from the crowd, "Blessed is the womb that bore you, and the breasts you sucked!" Jesus replied, "Blessed, rather, are those who hear the Word of God and keep it!" (Lk 11:27-28).

Our Lord surely did not intend, however, to *denigrate* His mother by this statement. Nor is it likely that St. Luke would contradict what he wrote earlier in his Gospel about Mary being supremely "blessed" among all women (see Lk 1:28, 42, 48). The Greek word translated "rather" in Jesus' saying in Luke 11 is the word *menoun*, which in this context means not "on the contrary," but "even more"; in other words: "even more blessed are those who hear the Word of God and keep it." The Protestant biblical scholar Margaret Thrall gives this same interpretation of the words of Jesus in her book *Greek Particles in the New Testament*. Thrall claims that Jesus intended to express Himself like this:

> What you have said is true as far as it goes. But the blessedness of Mary does not consist simply of the fact of her relationship towards myself, but (*menoun*) [even more] in the fact that she shares in the blessedness of those who hear the word of God and keep it, and it is in this that true blessedness lies.[10]

As we shall see later in this book, even before she was told by the angel that she would be the Mother of the Messiah, Mary was already well prepared by the Holy Spirit to fulfill her vocation as Mother of God. Saint Gregory Nazianzen in the fourth century taught that Mary was "pre-purified" before the coming of the angel. She was already "blessed" in a unique way by God. That is why, when the angel Gabriel first spoke to her, he called her "full of grace" (Lk 1:28). Commenting on these words of the angel, St. Sophronius of Jerusalem in the seventh century summed up the angel's meaning: "No one has been purified in advance as you."

In short, when Mary, the New Eve, received the Christ Child in her womb at the Annunciation, her Heart was already overflowing with grace, made ready in advance to surrender her life completely to the Lord. Being so completely prepared for her vocation by divine grace, therefore, she must have cooperated with that grace to an eminent degree, through her many years of intimate companionship and maternal loving care for her Son, attaining a truly unfathomable measure of holiness.[11]

What better example can be found in all of Scripture of someone who (to borrow our Lord's phrase) "heard the Word of God and kept it"? Mary, the New Eve, totally surrendered her life to God's Word, spoken by the angel, when she replied to him: "Behold, I am the handmaiden of the Lord. Let it be done to me according to your word" (Lk 1:38). Surely, Jesus was well aware of this fact when He said, "Even more blessed are those who hear the Word of God and keep it!" (Lk 11:28).

Finally, if Mary was not all-holy, completely surrendered to the Spirit of God throughout her entire life, then isn't there something missing from the Gospel story? Jesus said that the first commandment is to love God with "all your heart." But if Many did not do this, then who else ever did? No one, apparently — so the commandment God gave to the Israelites as the first and greatest of all was impassible to keep, and the prophecies implicit in the mystical love-poetry of the Song of Solomon will never be fulfilled: "You are all fair, my love. There is no flaw in you ... My dove, my perfect one, is only one" (Song 4:7, 6:9).

God does not give impossible commandments, or make false prophecies. There is one human person and only one who truly loved the Lord back with all her heart: Mary of Nazareth, the Mother of God.

PRAYER

O sweet Mother of God,
I model my life on You;
You are for me the bright dawn;
In You I lose myself, enraptured.

O Mother, Immaculate Virgin.
In You the divine ray is reflected,
Midst storms, 'tis You who teach me to love the Lord,
O my shield and defense from the foe.

(St. Maria Faustina Kowalska, *Diary*, 1232)

QUESTIONS FOR DISCUSSION

1. How does Mary's title "Mother of God" sum up the truth of the doctrine of the Incarnation?

2. Imagine Mary looking after Jesus as a little boy: How might she have grown in faith and love by being so close to Him?

3. Imagine Mary dwelling with Jesus in Nazareth when He was grown up until the time came for Him to start His ministry of preaching and healing in Galilee: How might she have grown even further in faith and love by having such a close relationship with Him for so many years? How can we grow in the love of Jesus by serving Him daily with love, even in small things?

SUGGESTIONS FOR FURTHER READING

- *Catechism of the Catholic Church*, entries 496-497

- Father Donald Calloway, MIC, *Under the Mantle*, pp. 15-19 and 270-271

CHAPTER FOUR

Mary,
Ever Virgin

There is no Catholic belief about Mary that sounds stranger to modern ears than the doctrine of Mary's "perpetual virginity." Virginity itself is something so denigrated in our culture today that young people are encouraged by the media and entertainment industry to lose their own virginity as quickly as possible! Few doctrines seem more difficult to appreciate, therefore, than the Catholic teaching that Mary remained a virgin before, during, and after the birth of her Son, Jesus.

The Tradition of the Church, however, is overwhelmingly in favor of this doctrine. In fact, this Tradition is so well established that even the great Protestant Reformers (Luther, Calvin, Zwingli, and, later, John Wesley), though they departed from the Catholic heritage on many things, yet retained their belief in Mary as the "Ever Virgin" Mother of the Savior.

Saints and Fathers, Popes and Councils

In the era of the ancient Church Fathers, St. Jerome claimed that the fourth-century heretic Helvidius was the first one ever to argue that Mary had other children after Jesus was born. Also in the fourth century, St. Epiphanius of Cyprus insisted that the mere fact that Christians everywhere referred to Mary as the "Blessed Virgin" was proof enough that the tradition of her perpetual virginity was a reliable one.

The early popes and councils also taught the doctrine of the perpetual virginity of Mary. Saint Pope Siricius, for example, explicitly endorsed this belief in 392 A.D. In the following century, St. Pope Leo the Great, in his famous work called the *Tome*, stated: "She [Mary] brought Him forth without the loss of virginity, even as she conceived Him without its loss … [Jesus Christ] was born from the Virgin's womb, because it was a miraculous birth." Leo's *Tome* was later confirmed by the bishops assembled at the Fourth Ecumenical Council of the Church at Chalcedon in 451 A.D. Then in 553 A.D., the bishops at the Fifth Ecumenical Council of the Church (the Second Council of

Constantinople) affirmed that the divine Son of God, "incarnate of the holy and glorious Mother of God and ever-virgin Mary, was born of her." Later, in 649 A.D., the threefold character of Mary's virginity was declared to be an article of faith by St. Pope Martin I:

> The blessed ever-virginal and immaculate Mary conceived, without seed, by the Holy Spirit, and without loss of integrity brought Him forth, and after His birth preserved her virginity inviolate.

In continuing to uphold the doctrine of the perpetual virginity of Mary, therefore, the Catholic Church today is doing no more than maintaining the consensus of the early Christian community. As the *Catechism of the Catholic Church* tells us (entry 499):

> The deepening of faith in the virginal motherhood led the Church to confess Mary's real and perpetual virginity even in the act of giving birth to the Son of God made man. In fact, Christ's birth "did not diminish his mother's virginal integrity but sanctified it." And so the liturgy of the Church celebrates Mary as *Aeiparthenos*, the "Ever-virgin."

Mary's Virginity Before the Birth of Jesus

Few Christians dispute the fact that Mary conceived Jesus in her womb by the Holy Spirit without human fatherhood, simply because this is the clear and explicit teaching of the New Testament (see Mt 1:18-25; Lk 1:26-56). Saint Matthew tells us that this virginal conception is a fulfillment of an Old Testament prophecy (see Is 7:14) as well as a sign of the true divinity of Christ: "Behold, a virgin shall conceive and bear a son, and his name shall be called Emmanuel (which means, God with us)."[12]

Mary's Virginity Preserved During the Birth of Jesus

The belief that Mary remained a virgin even during the birth of her Son, however, seems very strange to modern readers. Why were the early Christians so convinced of the truth of this doctrine? A good summary of their thinking is found in the 16th century in the Church's official *Catechism of the Council of Trent*, also known as *The Roman Catechism* (article 3):

> For in a way wonderful beyond expression or conception, he [Jesus] is born of his Mother without any diminution of her maternal virginity. As he afterwards went forth from the sepulcher while it was closed and sealed, and entered the room in which his disciples were assembled, although "the doors were closed" (Jn 20:19), or, not to depart from natural events which we witness every day, as the rays of the sun penetrate the substance of glass without breaking or injuring it in the least: so, but in a more incomprehensible manner, did Jesus Christ come forth from his mother's womb without injury to her maternal virginity ...
>
> To Eve it was said: "In pain you shall bring forth children" (Gen 3:16). Mary was exempt from this law, for preserving her virginal integrity inviolate, she brought forth Jesus the Son of God, without experiencing ... any sense of pain.

Here the *Roman Catechism* suggests two arguments for the preservation of Mary's virginity during childbirth. The first is the hint that, as the New Eve, she was so "full of grace" (Lk 1:28) that she must have been exempt from the divine decree of painful childbirth, a decree that was one of the consequences of the fall of Adam and Eve in the Garden of Eden (see Gen 3:16). As we shall see later, the words of the old *Catechism* here foreshadow the truth of another doctrine about Mary: her Immaculate Conception (that is, the doctrine that she was full of grace from the very moment of her conception, and thereby exempt from original sin and its effects).

Second, the *Roman Catechism* suggests that it is fitting that Mary's virginity should remain unbroken by the birth of Jesus. After all, her Son is the divine Son of God, sent into the world to heal mankind from sin, and from all its evil effects: guilt and punishment, suffering and death. *How could He who was sent for the healing of the world be born in a way that caused pain and bloodshed to His own mother?* The very manner of the birth of the Prince of Peace and the Beloved Physician, therefore, must be exempt from directly causing hurt and harm. Catholic theologian John Saward explained the matter like this:

> Why was it necessary for the Son of God to be born as man in a way that would not injure the integrity of His mother's virginity? The necessity is again one of fittingness, of harmony and thus of beauty, like the need to fit a third and a fifth alongside the root to achieve the lovely consonance of a major chord ... The miracle of the Virgin Birth is in wonderful harmony with the saving purposes of the Incarnation of the Word. St. Thomas [Aquinas] argues that ... as He [Jesus] enters Mary's womb, so He leaves it — without hurt or harm of its maidenly wholeness.[13]

Mary's Virginity Preserved After the Birth of Jesus

Finally, there is the doctrine that Mary remained a virgin throughout the rest of her life. In fact, only an original, lifelong commitment on Mary's part to preserve her virginity makes sense of the words that she spoke to the angel Gabriel. After being told by the angel that she would "conceive in her womb and bear a son," Mary replied, "How can this be, since I have no husband?" (Lk 1:34). Catholic biblical scholar Scott Hahn explains:

> Now this would be an odd question if Mary had planned to have normal marital relations with her

husband. The angel told her only that she would conceive a son, which is a commonplace event in marriage
... Mary should have known exactly "how this shall
be." It would happen in the normal course of nature.

But that, apparently, was beyond the realm of
possibility for her. The unspoken assumption behind
her question is that, even though she was betrothed,
she should not have an opportunity to conceive a
child ... Some commentators speculate that Mary
must have vowed virginity from an early age, and that
Joseph knew of her vow, accepted it, and eventually
took it on himself ... We do find examples of celibacy
in the time of Jesus, evidenced in the New Testament
by Jesus himself, and by St. Paul [also by St. John the
Baptist] ... The Dead Sea Scrolls attest that celibacy
was a common practice of some Israelite sects [such
as the Essenes at Qumran, and the Therapeutae community of Jewish women in Egypt]. So it was not
unthinkable that Mary could have vowed virginity.[14]

Besides, if Mary had conceived other children with Joseph
after the birth of Jesus, why do we hear no mention of them in
the story of the finding of Jesus in the Temple of Jerusalem in
Luke 2:41-51? Luke tells us that His parents spent three days
searching for Him all over the city (see 2:46): Where were His
(alleged) younger brothers and sisters during all that time? And
if Jesus really had younger siblings, why, when He was dying
on the Cross, did He entrust His mother into the care of the
Beloved Disciple, St. John, rather than into the care of her next
eldest son, according to Jewish family custom? (See Jn 19:25-27;
we will say more about this Scripture passage in Chapter Eight).
The evidence of the Gospel story suggests, therefore, that Mary
remained true to her vow of virginity throughout her life and,
along with St. Joseph, dedicated her entire life solely to her Son,
Jesus. As we shall see, the perpetual virginity of Mary is a clear
sign of her *total commitment and consecration* to Christ's work
of salvation.

Biblical Objections to Mary's Perpetual Virginity

Our Protestant brothers and sisters often express doubts about the doctrine of Mary's perpetual virginity, so we must take a close look at their objections, and look for ways in which their concerns might be addressed.

Quite often, Catholics will hear their Protestant friends and acquaintances express disbelief in this doctrine simply because the standard translations of the Bible they read explicitly mention the "brothers and sisters" of Jesus (for instance, Mt 12:46-50, 13:55; Mk 3:31-35). But we must not be misled by translated texts. The word "brother" in New Testament Greek had a broad range of meaning, much as it did in Hebrew and Aramaic at the time, and does even today in Arabic and Slavic languages, where one's "brother" can be any male relative of the same generation (including cousins and half-brothers). According to Protestant biblical scholar W.E. Vine, the New Testament Greek word "*adelphos*" (plural, *adelphoi*) can mean a "brother or near kinsman."[15]

Ancient Greek also had special words for "cousin" and "near relative" ("*anepsios*" and "*sungenis*"), but it is clear that the New Testament writers followed the custom of the Greek translation of the Old Testament, the version that they commonly read (called "the Septuagint"), and sometimes used *adelphos* for brother or near relative as well. Tim Staples explains why in his book *Behold Your Mother*:

> The apostles were Jews, and so they spoke (and wrote) Greek with a "Jewish accent." Since in Hebrew and Aramaic it was common to refer to all sorts of male relations as *brothers*, it is not surprising that when they spoke or wrote in Greek they tended to refer to all extended male relations as *brothers*. And so the real question is not whether Greek has a word for *cousin* or not. The question should be: Did first-century Jews — and the authors of Sacred Scripture here in

question, who were Jewish converts — use the Greek word for *brother* the same way they used its Hebrew and Aramaic equivalents?

The answer to the above is a definitive yes. In the Septuagint ... we have multiple examples [Staples cites Lev 10:4, 1 Chr 23:22, and Tobit 7:2-4] ... They chose to use *adelphos* as well ... for *cousin* or *relative* as well as for *brother*.[16]

The early tradition of the Church actually gives us two ways of understanding who these "brothers and sisters" of Jesus really were. The explanation favored by the *Catechism* (entry 500) is based on connecting the dots among several New Testament passages. It is also based on the testimony of St. Jerome (d. 420 A.D.), a scholar who lived most of his life in Palestine and was an expert in Hebrew, Greek, and Latin, as well as in the ancient biblical texts. Jerome insisted that the "brothers and sisters" of Jesus were actually His cousins, children of another "Mary" mentioned in Scripture, one called "the wife of Clopas," probably the Blessed Virgin Mary's own cousin. David Armstrong explains this in his book *A Biblical Defense of Catholicism*:

> By comparing Matthew 27:56, Mark 15:40, and John 19:25, we find that James and Joseph — mentioned in Matthew 13:55 with Simon and Jude as Jesus' "brothers" — are also called sons of Mary, the wife of Clopas. This other Mary (Matt 27:61, 28:1) is called our Lady's adelphe in Jn 1:25 (it isn't likely that there were two women named "Mary" in the same [nuclear] family — thus, even this usage apparently means "cousin" or more distant relative). Matthew 13:55-56 and Mark 6:3 mention Simon, Jude, and "sisters" along with James and Joseph, calling all adelphoi. Since we know for sure that at least James and Joseph are not Jesus' blood brothers, the most likely interpretation of Mt. 13:35 is that all these brothers are "cousins," according to linguistic conventions.[17]

Another early Christian explanation for the identity of these "brothers and sisters" of Jesus was that they were children of St. Joseph by a previous marriage. Joseph was said to be a widower, and his children from his first marriage would have been half-brothers and half-sisters of Jesus. This fits with a common use of the word *adelphoi* at the time (see, for example, Mt 14:3, where Herod's half-brother Philip is called his *adelphos*). It also could explain why Jesus is referred to in St. Mark's Gospel only as "son of Mary" and never as "son of Joseph." In Nazareth, Jesus would have been known around the town as "the son of Mary" rather than in the normal, Jewish way as the son of His earthly father, simply in order to distinguish Him from the children of Joseph by his first wife. This was a common Old Testament naming custom. In fact, this way of understanding "the brothers and sisters" of Jesus was taken for granted by all the second-century writings that attempted to tell the story of our Lord's early family life. Clearly, it was not something these later writers invented, but rather something they just passed on to their readers as if everyone already knew it to be true. It was accepted by the Fathers of the Eastern Church as well, and remains to this day the general belief of Eastern Orthodox Christians.

What is common to both of these traditions? Whether the "brothers and sisters" of Jesus were really His cousins (as Western Christianity has held) or His half-brothers and half-sisters (as Eastern Christianity has held), in neither case are they biological children of the Blessed Virgin Mary. Early Church Tradition, therefore, both East and West, is unanimous that Jesus was the only child of Mary.

Some Scripture commentators argue that the word "until" in Mt 1:25 ("Joseph ... knew her not until she had borne a son") implies that Mary and Joseph had conjugal relations after Jesus was born. But as the *Ignatius Catholic Study Bible: New Testament* points out:

> The Greek *heos* [until] does not imply that Joseph and Mary had marital relations following Jesus' birth. This conjunction is often used (translated "to" or "til") to indicate a select period of time, without implying a change in the future (2 Sam 6:23 [Septuagint]; Jn

9:18; 1 Tim 4:13). Here Matthew emphasizes only that Joseph had no involvement in Mary's pregnancy *before* Jesus' birth.[18]

Other commentators claim that the phrase "first-born son" used for Jesus (see Mt 1:25; Lk 2:7) *must* imply that Mary had additional sons (a second-born, a third born, etc.) after Jesus was born. But as Mark Miravalle explains, that is simply not what the Jewish phrase "first-born" actually meant at the time:

> The term "first-born son" neither infers nor establishes that other children were born later. In Mosaic Law the term "first-born" was applied to the child whose birth had not been *preceded* by another, regardless of whether other children followed or not. According to the Law, every mother was required to go through certain rituals after the birth of her first child (whether followed by other children or not).[19]

Mary's Perpetual Virginity and Her Total Consecration to God

For some Catholics, an obstacle to belief in Mary's perpetual virginity arises from the fact that the refusal of Mary and Joseph to consummate their marriage would seem to imply (in accordance with Catholic teaching) that they were not validly married at all! However, in God's plan, conjugal relations in marriage are really a means to an end: given to spouses by God as a way for them to express, strengthen, and celebrate their total self-gift to each other, and as an act that opens their marriage, their lives, and their hearts to the gift of children. Mary and Joseph, however, received the gift of a child from God in a special, miraculous manner. Moreover, by the Holy Spirit, Mary ("full of grace," according to Lk 1:28) and Joseph (a truly "just man," according to Mt 1:19) doubtless had already attained in their hearts the total gift of themselves to each other. There already existed a union of hearts between them, in the Holy Spirit, of a depth that can be found only among the saints in Heaven. Conjugal union, therefore, was needed neither to strengthen this self-gift nor to enable them to have a child. In short, for this special couple to agree to offer their capacity for conjugal union as a gift to God to enable them more freely to dedicate their entire lives to their divine Son does not constitute any impediment to the reality of their marriage.

Among many non-Catholics, the "strangeness" of the doctrine of Mary's perpetual virginity consists in the suspicion that it stems from a generally negative attitude toward human sexuality in the Catholic tradition, a defect allegedly stretching back to the earliest centuries of the Church. The claim is that sex was always seen by the Catholic Church as something sinful or worldly, too tied up with the body, and therefore a distraction from things pertaining to the human spirit and to eternal life.

Indeed, there have been times and places in Catholic history, such as late Antiquity and the early Middle Ages, where a relatively anti-body and anti-sex mentality seemed to prevail. First-century Palestine, however — the world of Mary, Joseph, and the Apostolic writers of the New Testament — was not one of them. In that time, and especially among the Jews, conjugal relations between husband and wife were generally held to be good and wholesome, a created gift of God for the procreation of creatures in His own "image" (see Gen 1:26-27). Besides, the Catholic Church has always held that Holy Matrimony is one of the Sacraments of the Church — hardly the kind of belief compatible with a thoroughly anti-body and anti-sex religion.

Catholic scholar Roch Kereszty, OCist, explains that even in the age of the later Church Fathers (several centuries after the Apostolic Era) when relatively negative attitudes toward human sexuality were more widespread, the Fathers generally did not argue that Mary must have preserved her virginity in order to keep her from any imagined "evil" of sexual intercourse:

> The patristic argument for the perpetual virginity of Mary is ... based on the understanding of virginity as *a total consecration to God in pure faith and undivided love.* They interpret Lk 1:34 as expressing the firm intention (or vow) of Mary to dedicate herself to

God as a virgin; such a dedication must be total and irrevocable. They also see in the womb of Mary the New Ark of God overshadowed by the Holy Spirit, the New Temple forever sanctified by God's presence. No man may enter that sanctuary since God has made it his own [see Ezek 44:1-3].[20]

Let's look at this passage from Ezekiel more closely. In Ezekiel 44, the prophet was given a vision of the Temple that would one day be rebuilt in Jerusalem, and an explanation of the significance of the east gate of that Temple:

Then he brought me back to the outer gate of the sanctuary, which faces east; and it was shut. And he said to me, "This gate shall remain shut; it shall not be opened and no one shall enter by it; for the Lord, the God of Israel, has entered by it; therefore it shall remain shut.

Why did the ancient Fathers of the Church see in this "east gate" a symbol of the total consecration to God of the Virgin Mary? Because in John 2:19, Jesus calls Himself — to be precise, He calls His body — the true Temple of the Lord. So if Jesus' body is the true fulfilment of Ezekiel's vision of the Temple in Ezekiel 44, then who or what is the "east gate" through which the Lord enters that Temple? Mary is the true and natural fulfilment of this prophecy, for it was in her womb that the Lord entered His Temple — that is, united Himself with human flesh — in the Incarnation. Like the east gate, Mary's womb, *specially consecrated to God for His use alone*, is always to remain shut. As St. Jerome wrote back in the fourth century:

Only Christ opened the doors of the virginal womb, which continued to remain closed, however. This is the closed eastern gate, through which only the high priest may enter and exit and which nevertheless is always closed.[21]

Our Protestant brothers and sisters naturally want to know where we get this whole idea of "total consecration to God" in the form of "consecrated virginity." "Where in the Bible do you find that?" they ask. As Catholics, we need to remember that most Protestant churches do not have a tradition of celibate priests or of consecrated virgins living under vows in "religious life," so the whole notion of this special vocation in the Church can be hard for Protestants to grasp at first.

The idea of consecrated virginity, however, appears in several places in the Bible. It was not entirely unknown to the Jews, who already had the example from ancient times of the divinely commanded celibacy of the prophet Jeremiah (see Jer 16:1-4). Jesus spoke of those specially called by God to embrace a life of celibacy, referring to them metaphorically as "eunuchs" for the sake of the service of His Kingdom (see Mt 19:10-12). Saint Paul also wrote of a special Christian calling to virginity, embraced in order to serve God with an undivided heart (see 1 Cor 7:1-8, 32-35). He even gives instructions to his missionary delegate Timothy about how to guide and govern the early Christian widows who had consecrated the remainder of their lives to God in celibacy (see 1 Tim 5:5, 9-12). As we shall see in the next chapter of this book, the Heart of Mary, full of divine grace, was more completely dedicated to the Kingdom of Jesus Christ than the heart of any other creature — so she likely would have embraced the way of life that best enabled her to remain *totally consecrated to Him, dedicated to Him alone.*

Even the whole notion of "consecrating" someone or something to God may sound foreign to non-Catholic ears. Once again, however, the notion is entirely biblical. In Scripture, to "consecrate" someone or something to God was to set it apart for God, for His exclusive and holy use. For example, the Old Testament Law is filled with references to aspects of Jewish worship that were set aside for holy use alone: the priests (see Ex 29:1-9), the priestly garments (see Ex 28:40-43), the offerings (see Ex 29:31-34) the sanctuary (see 2 Chr 30:8), the Ark of the Covenant (see Num 4:17-20), and the Nazirite vow (see Jg 13:3-5). To use any of these consecrated things for anything other than a holy use was considered a sacrilege. In the New Testament, St. Paul twice has his head shaved as a sign of his special vow of consecration to God (see Acts 18:18 and 21:23-24).

The Blessed Virgin Mary was chosen and set apart by God, with her consent, for the most important holy purpose of all. Tim Staples explains in *Behold Your Mother*:

> Our Blessed Mother was consecrated to God in the context of a nuptial union with God [in other words, to be, in a sense, the spouse of the Holy Spirit] for the specific and sacred purpose of bringing Christ into the world for the salvation of all ...
>
> In Scripture, once something or someone is consecrated or set apart for God's use, often accompanied by sacred vows, the thing or person so consecrated is generally not to be used for anything else. This has obvious implications for Mary's perpetual virginity. If Mary was consecrated to God in a nuptial union in order to bring forth Christ, there would be no question of Joseph's ever having conjugal relations with her.[22]

Saint Jerome summed it up best:

> Would he [St. Joseph], who knew such great wonders, have dared to touch the temple of God, the dwelling place of the Holy Spirit, the Mother of His Lord?[23]

All this is not to say, of course, that Mary and Joseph lacked real marital affection for each other; surely their affection for each other was more exalted by grace in love and tenderness than any other purely human spousal relationship could ever be! And no doubt it was expressed in appropriate hugs, kisses, and caresses just as with all authentic spousal love. They were not bodiless creatures, after all, but expressed their love for each other through their bodies. At the same time, they were full of wonder at the deep mystery of the special consecration of Mary's body in God's plan, a mystery that both would have respected and cherished. Joseph and Mary could be so closely bonded to each other in tenderness and love precisely because, first and foremost, they were so completely consecrated to God.

PRAYER

Holiest Virgin, with all my heart I venerate you above all the angels and saints in paradise as the Daughter of the Eternal Father, and I consecrate to you my soul with all its powers.

Holiest Virgin, with all my heart I venerate you above all the angels and saints in paradise as the Mother of the only-begotten Son, and I consecrate to you my body with all its senses.

Holiest Virgin, with all my heart I venerate you above all the angels and saints in paradise as the beloved Spouse of the Holy Spirit, and I consecrate to you my heart and all its affections, praying to you to obtain for me from the Most Holy Trinity all the graces I need for my salvation. Amen.

(Fr. Lawrence Lovasik, SVD)

QUESTIONS FOR DISCUSSION

1. What is the significance of the doctrine that Mary conceived Jesus in her womb while she was a virgin, by the Holy Spirit, without human fatherhood?

2. Why does the Church teach that Mary's virginity remained unbroken even during the birth of Jesus?

3. Why does the Church believe that Mary remained a virgin even after the birth of Jesus, and throughout her entire life?

4. How can we describe the significance of consecrated virginity in the service of God in Scripture and Catholic Tradition?

SUGGESTIONS FOR FURTHER READING

- Matthew 1:18-25

- *Catechism*, entries 496-507

CHAPTER FIVE

Mary's Immaculate Conception

Our Evangelical brothers and sisters sometimes say to us:

> It may be that the titles given to Mary by the early Church — New Eve, Mother of God, and Ever Virgin — can be justified from Scripture. But the Bible also tells us that God's plan of salvation was to rescue the world by His grace alone, through *His Son Jesus alone*, and not through anyone else's good works, not even those of His mother Mary!

Now, in a sense, Catholics do not really disagree with that. The Church has always taught that we cannot do any good deeds at all that lead us even one step closer to salvation apart from divine grace. The same holds true for Mary. She did not cooperate with God's plan of salvation for the world by some personal effort all her own; rather, she was prompted, assisted, and strengthened to surrender to God's will every step of the way by His grace. In fact, Catholics believe that everything good in Mary's Heart and everything good that she ever did was the result of God's grace working within her and through her, from the first moment of her existence until the day she was enthroned at the side of her Son as Queen of Heaven and on into eternity. This doctrine that Mary's Heart was full of grace from the very beginning of her life is called the doctrine of her "Immaculate Conception."

What Does the "Immaculate Conception" Really Mean?

According to the *Catechism of the Catholic Church* (entries 491-492):

> Through the centuries the Church has become ever more aware that Mary, "full of grace" through God, was redeemed from the first moment of her conception. That is what the dogma of the Immaculate

Conception confesses, as Pope Pius IX proclaimed in 1854:

> The most Blessed Virgin Mary was, from the first moment of her conception, by a singular grace and privilege of almighty God and in virtue of the merits of Jesus Christ, Savior of the human race, preserved immune from all stain of original sin.

> "The splendor of an entirely unique holiness" by which Mary is "enriched from the first instant of her conception" comes wholly from Christ: she is "redeemed, in a more excellent fashion, by reason of the merits of her Son."

The "Immaculate Conception," therefore, means that from the first moment of her existence, Mary's soul was preserved from the effects of the fall of Adam and Eve, which means she was "full of grace" right from the start. This special gift was given to her on the basis of the merits of the life, Death, and Resurrection of Jesus Christ. Since God exists beyond all time, and all times are present before Him, He can apply the graces of Christ's redemptive work to people living at any time in human history (for instance, 1 Cor 10:4). It was on this basis that He poured out graces upon the patriarchs and prophets even before the coming of the Savior. He did so for Mary, too — but uniquely, in her case, right from the moment of her conception.

Our Evangelical brothers and sisters object that this Catholic doctrine seems to imply that Mary was not redeemed from sin by Jesus Christ. In his book *Know and Defend What You Love*, however, Fr. Adolf Faroni shows that this is not the case at all. Following the teachings of the great Franciscan theologian Blessed John Duns Scotus, Faroni writes:

> An objection to the Immaculate Conception of Mary claims that Mary cannot be immaculate, otherwise she would not have been redeemed by Jesus. This would detract from the universality of the redemption of Jesus, the only Mediator between God and men (1

Tm 2:5), in whom alone there is salvation (cf. Acts 4:12). Mary herself calls God her "Savior" (Lk 1:47).

The objection shows a fundamental misconception that to be full of grace means absence of redemption. On the contrary, it *implies* redemption because Mary's fullness of grace is the fruit of the saving death of Christ ... Mary has been redeemed like us, only in a more wonderful way, not by cure but by prevention. A doctor can save our life by curing sickness. But if He gives us a medicine that keeps us from getting sick, He saves us much better.[24]

That God has the power to preserve people from sin is clearly stated in the Bible. Saint Jude tells us that God has the power to preserve any baptized Christian from sin, if only we will surrender completely to His merciful love: "Now to him who is able to keep you from falling and to present you without blemish before the presence of his glory, to him the only God, our Savior through Jesus Christ our Lord, be glory, majesty, dominion and authority, before all time and now and forever. Amen" (Jude 24-25).

In fact, God often gives extraordinary graces to those to whom He entrusts extraordinary responsibilities. Thus, Jeremiah was called and consecrated to be a prophet of the Lord from before his birth; Moses, who was to lead the Jews out of slavery and into the Promised Land, encountered the Lord in a burning bush, and St. Paul, who was to become the great "Apostle to the Gentiles," was struck blind and converted on the road to Damascus by a vision of the risen Christ. Mary was given a special grace, too — the gift of an outpouring of grace in her soul from the moment of her origin — in order to prepare her for her special vocation: the unique responsibility of being the Mother of God Incarnate. As Blessed John Henry Newman once wrote:

By original sin we mean ... something negative, that is, the deprivation of that supernatural, unmerited grace which Adam and Eve had on their first formation — deprivation and the consequences of deprivation. Mary could not merit, any more than they, the restoration of that grace; but it was restored to her by God's free bounty, from the first moment of her existence, and thereby, in fact, she never came under the original curse, which consisted in the loss of it. And she had this special privilege in order to fit her to become the Mother of her and our Redeemer, to fit her ... spiritually for it. So that, by the aid of the first grace, she might grow in grace, that, when the angel came and her Lord was at hand, she might be "full of grace," prepared as far as a creature could be prepared to receive him into her bosom.[25]

Biblical Roots of the Doctrine

The Catholic Church does not claim that the doctrine of the Immaculate Conception can be proven from Scripture *alone*. This does not worry Catholics at all, however, because the Bible itself never says that Scripture is the only source of divinely revealed truth. Indeed, quite the opposite is the case (see, for example, 2 Thess 2:15 and 1 Tim 3:15). Just as we see the world around us most clearly when we look through both of our physical eyes at once, rather than just through one eye, in the same way we need to look with the eyes of *both* Scripture and Tradition in order to see clearly what God has revealed to us through Christ and His apostles. Although not explicitly taught by Scripture, the doctrine of the Immaculate Conception has its roots in the Bible. Several biblical passages point in the direction of Mary's uniquely graced origin, and taken together, they provide us with strong evidence for the Immaculate Conception, even before we add to it the witness of Sacred Tradition.

Two passages in the Bible in particular contain the seeds of this wonderful doctrine. First, in Genesis 3:15, after the fall of Adam and Eve, the Lord says to the serpent that tempted them, "I will put enmity between you and the woman, and between your seed and her seed; he shall bruise your head, and you shall bruise his heel."

This Old Testament passage is the first prophecy of the Gospel, which is why the ancient Fathers of the Church called it the *protoevangelium* ("first Gospel"). Here the "seed" of the woman who will crush the "serpent's" head (that is, the devil's head) can only be Jesus Christ, who is to crush Satan victoriously by His work of redemption. It follows that "the woman" prophesied in this same passage must be the Mother of Jesus, the Blessed Virgin Mary (see Jn 2:4 and 19:26 where Jesus mysteriously calls her "woman"). In Genesis 3, both Jesus and Mary are said to be in a state of "enmity" against the serpent, which in the original Hebrew means "complete and radical opposition" to him. It is for this reason that it is not likely that God would have permitted Mary to inherit the condition of original sin from Adam and Eve. Any participation by her in the disorder and corruption of the soul that the rest of us inherit from Adam and Eve would place the mother of Jesus at least partially under the sway of Satan and evil, and thereby contradict the complete "enmity" between Mary and Satan prophesied in Genesis 3.

The second Bible passage that points to the truth of the Immaculate Conception is Luke 1:28, the words of the angel Gabriel to Mary at the Annunciation: "Hail, full of grace." (In the original Greek of the New Testament, we read the word *kecharitomene*, that is, "full of grace.") In this passage, "full of grace" is used as a name or title for Mary, and she is the only one addressed in this fashion in the entire Bible, so it must indicate something special and distinctive about her.

Some modern versions of the Bible translate this passage as "Hail, O favored one," but that is not an entirely accurate translation. The root word of *kecharitomene* is the Greek word *charis*, which is usually translated into English as "grace." The English word "favor" can refer merely to an external gift or honor of some kind, but God's highest "favors" are never merely external honors or gifts: An interior gracing of some kind is always involved. Thus, in this passage of Scripture, Mary is said to have been "graced" in some interior, spiritual sense.

Some Bible commentators argue that by using the word *kecharitomene*, the angel only meant that Mary was being "graced" in the sense that, at that very moment, she was called to be the Mother of the Savior. However, the angel Gabriel went on to say in verse 30, "Do not be afraid, Mary, for you have found favor with God." This implies that she had already been graced in some special way in the past. It is on that basis alone — on the basis of that earlier divine gift of grace — that she had "found favor," and was now being called by God to her special vocation.

In fact, the word *kecharitomene* ("full of grace") that the angel used for Mary is neither in the present nor the future tense: It is a *perfect passive participle*. This verbal form signifies an action completed in the past, with ongoing effects in the present. In other words, the angel spoke of a gift that Mary had already received in the past, and that was still in effect at that very moment. The angel literally says to her: "Hail, graced one."

The only other place in the entire New Testament where the same Greek verb form, *charitoo*, is used is in Ephesians 1:6. We know from the Greek-speaking Church Father St. John Chrysostom (347-407 A.D.) that in that particular passage, the verb *charitoo* means to be completely "transformed by grace," and he implies that this is the common meaning of the word.[26] Thus, the most accurate translation of the angel Gabriel's salutation to Mary would be: "Hail, transformed-by-grace-one, the Lord is with you!"[27]

What could such a complete transformation by the grace of God consist in other than a plenitude of sanctifying grace, poured into Mary's Heart from the Holy Spirit, right from the start of her personal existence? As the *Catechism* puts it (entry 492), she was "enriched from the first instant of her conception" with "the splendor of an entirely unique holiness." Saint John the Baptist was sanctified by the Holy Spirit in his mother's womb, according to Luke 1:15. Is it likely that Mary would receive a lesser grace to prepare her for her role as Mother of the Savior than John did in preparation for his special ministry?

Mary Immaculate and the Ancient Fathers of the Church

As we discussed earlier in this book (in Chapter Two), many of the earliest Fathers of the Church taught that Mary is the Second Eve. Just as Jesus is called by St. Paul the New Adam, the Head of redeemed humanity, so the Blessed Virgin Mary must be the

New Eve. There was no disagreement among the Fathers at all on this point. As Eve, the Mother of All the Living, had ushered in the age of sin by succumbing to the temptation of the fallen angel (the serpent), so Mary, the Mother of All the Redeemed, reversed Eve's sin by her obedience to the angel Gabriel at the Annunciation, and thereby ushered in the dawn of our salvation.

We should notice what this doctrine of the ancient Fathers of the Church implies. Eve began her life and vocation as "mother of all living" (Gen 3:20) in a state of innocence and grace, without any wound or corruption of original sin in her soul. Can we imagine that the Blessed Virgin Mary, whose vocation was to be the Mother of the Redeemer and of all the redeemed, received a lesser degree of grace in preparation for her singular vocation? As Blessed John Henry Newman once wrote:

> I ask, was not Mary as fully endowed [with grace] as Eve? Is it any violent inference that she, who was to cooperate in the redemption of the world, at least was not less endowed with power from on high than she who, given as helpmate to her husband, did in the event but cooperate with him for its ruin? If Eve was raised above human nature by that indwelling moral gift we call grace, is it rash to say that Mary had a greater grace? And this consideration gives significance to the angel's salutation to her as "full of grace" — an interpretation of the original word which is undoubtedly the right one as soon as we resist the common Protestant assumption that grace is mere external approbation and acceptance, answering to the word "favor," whereas it is, as the Fathers teach, a real inward condition or super-added quality of soul. And if Eve had this supernatural inward gift given her from the first moment of her personal existence, is it possible to deny too that Mary had this gift from the very first moment of her personal existence? I do not know how to resist this inference — well, this is simply and literally the doctrine of the Immaculate Conception. I say the doctrine of the Immaculate Conception is in substance this, and nothing more or less than this ...

and it really does seem to me to be bound up in that doctrine of the Fathers, that Mary is the Second Eve.[28]

Saint Ephrem the Syrian, writing in the fourth century (ca. 350 A.D.), summed up this great mystery for us:

> These two innocent ... women, Mary and Eve, had been [created] utterly equal, but afterwards one became the cause of our death, the other the cause of our life ...You [Jesus] and your Mother are the only ones who are immune from all stain; for there is no spot in You, O Lord, nor any taint in Your Mother.[29]

Scholars of the early Church also have discovered the text of a fourth-century homily, *On the Annunciation to the Mother of God and Against the Impious Arius*, attributed to a monk and disciple of St. Basil of Caesarea writing around the year 370. This document contains a most remarkable testimony to early Christian belief in the unique holiness of Mary:

> And so the angel arrived at the Virgin Mary's home, and having entered said to her: *Rejoice, full of grace!* He greeted her, his fellow servant, as if she were a great lady ... you who have been made worthy to provide a dwelling for such a lord ... you have become the most pure workshop of the divine economy; you have appeared as the worthy chariot for our king's entrance into life; you have been proclaimed the treasure, the spiritual pearl. *Blessed are you among women ...*
>
> *Do not fear, Mary, for you have found favor with God.* You have been made the most beautiful part of creation, more luminous than the heavens, more resplendent than the sun, higher than the angels. You were not lifted up into heaven, and yet, remaining on earth, you have drawn down into yourself the heavenly Lord and King of all.[30]

From the fifth century, the liturgies of the Christians of the East hailed the Blessed Virgin as *Panagia* ("all-holy one"), *Achranatos* ("the one without even the slightest stain"), and

Hypereulogoumene ("the one blessed beyond all others"). How could Mary be called *all*-holy, without *any* stain if, from the first moment of her existence, her soul lacked a complete outpouring of the Holy Spirit and sanctifying grace, and she carried within her soul instead the disorder, corruption, and inclination to sin that is passed down to all the rest of us from Adam and Eve?

Implicit in the teachings of the Fathers and early Liturgies of the Church, therefore, is the doctrine of Mary's fullness of grace, as the New Eve, right from the start of her personal existence: in other words, her Immaculate Conception.[31]

While many "Eastern Orthodox" Christians today (for instance, Greek, Russian, and Serbian Orthodox) do not accept the doctrine of Mary's original grace, the belief actually persisted in the East for many centuries, and was only widely rejected by Orthodox Christians in the 19th century. The great 14th-century Byzantine theologian Nicholas Cabasilas, for example, wrote about this mystery in his *Homily on the Nativity of Mary*: "If some holy doctors [i.e. ancient Fathers of the Church] said that the Virgin had been previously purified by the Spirit, we must believe they understood this purification in the sense of augmentation of graces. Nothing in her demanded purification."[32] Even in the 19th century, the famous Russian hermit and *starets* (spiritual father) St. Seraphim of Sarov upheld belief in Mary's graced origin.

Oddly enough, the doctrine of Mary's unique grace and holiness from the moment of conception even has roots in early *Protestant* tradition! The reformer Martin Luther, for example, had this to say about Our Lady's original grace in his *Personal Prayer Book* of 1522:

> [Mary] is full of grace, proclaimed to be entirely without sin ... God's grace fills her with everything good and makes her devoid of all evil. ... God is with her, meaning all she did or left undone is divine and the action of God in her. Moreover, God protected her from all that might be hurtful to her.

While the Protestant reformers of the 16th century were quick to abandon some Catholic doctrines, such as the authority of the pope and the sacrifice of the Mass, it is interesting that they clung to some Catholic traditions about Mary a lot longer. And in this case, it is not hard to see why ...

The Immaculate Conception
Proclaims Divine Mercy

Following in the footsteps of St. Paul, Protestant Evangelicals traditionally have sought to show how every mystery of the faith expresses the saving mercy of God. "To know Christ is to know His benefits," the early Lutheran theologians liked to say. In other words, speculative theology is of little value if its conclusions fail to glorify God's free grace and mercy. And yet, properly understood, that is precisely what Mary's Immaculate Conception magnifies most of all!

After all, what is Divine Mercy? It is God's undeserved, unmerited, often even unsought for divine grace — the grace that our compassionate God pours out upon us to help us overcome our miseries and meet our true needs.

Theologians call one form of that mercy God's "prevenient" grace, which means to "come before." In other words, even before we ask for it, and quite apart from the fact that we do not deserve it and have not earned it in the least, God graciously takes the initiative and comes to our aid. Prevenient grace is this completely free gift of God's mercy. We see a faint reflection of it in a parent's love for a child. A child is loved by its parents, not because the child has earned it or even asked for it in any way, but rather, the parent's love comes right from the start, a completely free gift, just because the child is the parent's own. That is human mercy "par excellence," and it is a mirror image of the divine.

When you think about it, that is exactly what is on display in the Immaculate Conception of the Blessed Virgin Mary. The Immaculate Conception is really the supreme manifestation of God's prevenient, unmerited mercy. After all, Mary did not "merit" her Immaculate Conception. Nor could she ask for it. It was something done in her and for her by the Father of Mercy, and solely on the basis of the foreseen merits of His Incarnate

Son, Jesus Christ. Saint John Paul II wrote in his encyclical *Dives in Misericordia* (*Rich in Mercy*, section 9): "Mary is the one who experienced mercy in an exceptional way — as no one else." Father Seraphim Michalenko, MIC, once explained the matter this way:

> The mystery of the Immaculate Conception ... is the expression of the first act of the heavenly Father's mercy in Mary's regard — an act of absolute gratuity. This is why we can see in it the Father's mercy in its pure state. The first act is the Father's prevenient mercy for this very tiny child that is to be born.

In fact, we can go further and say that the Immaculate Conception of the Blessed Virgin Mary was the great divine act of grace that lay at the foundation of God's whole work of salvation through Christ. The Father of Mercy took the initiative with sinful mankind, fashioning Mary's soul from the moment of conception, preserving it from the effects of original sin, making her soul the very masterpiece of His mercy, and it was this unique and extraordinary foundation of grace in Mary's soul that enabled her, years later, to respond to the angel Gabriel's message with total, trustful surrender: "Here am I, the servant of the Lord; let it be with me according to your word."

By God's prevenient grace, therefore, she was made the masterpiece of the Father's mercy. And in the fullness of time, this special grace enabled her to receive our Savior into the world. In short, the whole world's salvation began with a foundational act of unmerited, unprompted, freely-given Divine Mercy. That act of mercy was Mary's Immaculate Conception.

For this reason, it is hardly surprising that God chose the American branch of the Congregation of Marian Fathers of the Immaculate Conception to be the principal agents of the worldwide spread of the great message and devotion to the Divine Mercy that springs from the life and witness of St. Maria Faustina Kowalska (1905-1938). Her own religious congregation, the Sisters of Our Lady of Mercy, was trapped behind the Iron Curtain in Poland during the era of Communist rule of Eastern Europe, and therefore could not spread the message and devotion themselves.

A Gift For All

In his book *Mary's Journey*, Fr. Louis Cameli explains how the doctrine of the Immaculate Conception tells us something about our own Christian journey:

> We can speak of a combined celebration taking place on the Solemnity of the Immaculate Conception. We celebrate who Mary is through a unique gift of God, and who we are by reason of a similar gift …
>
> We are saved or redeemed from original sin when we are baptized and make our profession of faith in Jesus Christ. Mary was saved or redeemed by being preserved from original sin from the first moment of her conception … The way God moved in Mary's life from the very moment of her conception is similar to the way he moves in our lives. The Church's journey of faith with Mary brings us to a deeper understanding of the way God works in our lives.[33]

Father Cameli is reminding us here that if we were baptized as infants, then we experienced God's "prevenient grace" in a way that is somewhat similar to Mary's original grace at the moment of her conception. In each case, God reaches out and touches our lives without any prior merit, or effort on our part. And just as He did this for Mary to prepare her for her vocation, so His "prevenient" grace does something similar for every Christian, to prepare each one of us for the work He would have us do. Saint Paul tells us that this is the authentic pattern of God's grace in our lives: "For we are his workmanship, created in Christ Jesus for good works, which God prepared beforehand, that we should walk in them" (Eph 2:10).

The doctrine of the Immaculate Conception, however, also tells us something about Mary that is unique to her. On the great Solemnity on December 8 each year, Catholics celebrate the fact that by her Immaculate Conception, Mary was prepared for her special vocation as the Mother of our Savior. Her Immaculate

Conception is, thereby, a sign of God's free grace, making her the true dawn of salvation for the world and the cause of our joy. All of us are called to "honor your mother and father," according to the Ten Commandments. The divine Son of God honored His earthly mother in a special way by pouring His grace into her Heart from the first moment of her life.

As disciples of Jesus, called to follow Him in everything, let us also honor His mother by celebrating God's special gift to her, Mary's "Immaculate Conception," her "original grace." After all, it was given to her, not just for herself, but for the good of the whole world, for with the aid of this grace Mary welcomed the Christ Child into the world for the salvation of us all.

PRAYER

> Father, You prepared the Virgin Mary to be the worthy Mother of Your Son. You made it possible for her to share beforehand in the salvation Your Son Jesus Christ would bring by His death, and kept her without sin from the first moment of her conception. Give us the grace by her prayers to live in Your presence without sin. We ask this through the same Christ our Lord. Amen.
>
> (Fr. Lawrence Lovasik, SVD)

QUESTIONS FOR DISCUSSION

1. Why did God give to Mary the special grace of the Immaculate Conception?

2. What is the connection between the teaching of the early Christians that Mary is the New Eve, and the doctrine that Mary began her earthly life "full of grace"?

3. Mary's "original grace" was a free gift given to her right from the start of her life. What are some of the

free and unmerited gifts that God has given you, from your childhood until the present? What gifts did He give you especially to prepare you for your own particular vocation?

SUGGESTIONS FOR FURTHER READING

- *Catechism*, entries 487-493

- The opening section of Fr. Donald Calloway, MIC's book *Under the Mantle* entitled "The Woman of Our Dreams" pp. 15-21, in which he discusses the plenitude of gifts and graces that the Blessed Trinity poured out upon Mary

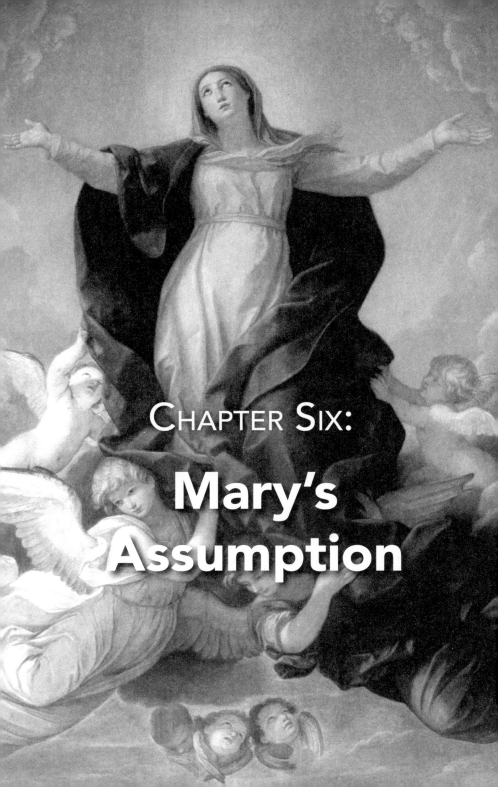

Chapter Six:

Mary's Assumption

On August 15 each year, Catholics celebrate a feast day in honor of one of the greatest mysteries of the life of the Blessed Virgin Mary: her bodily Assumption into Heaven. As the *Catechism of the Catholic Church* teaches:

> The Most Blessed Virgin Mary, when the course of her earthly life was completed, was taken up body and soul into the glory of heaven, where she already shares in the glory of her Son's Resurrection, anticipating the resurrection of all members of His Body (974).

In his book *Mysteries of the Virgin Mary*, Fr. Peter John Cameron, OP, recounts how the great French Catholic preacher Bossuet beautifully introduced this mystery of our faith. Bossuet said that Mary's passing away from this life "was wrought simply by the gradual perfecting of her love, which ... at last reached such perfection that an earthly body could no longer contain it ... Even as the lightest touch will make a ripe fruit drop from its stem, so was this perfect spirit gathered in one moment to its heavenly home, without effort or shock."[34] And at the same time or soon afterward, her body, our Savior's first home on earth, was glorified and united with her soul forever in Heaven.

Non-Catholics often ask: "Is there really any evidence at all that Mary was taken to Heaven body and soul at the end of her life, since the Bible seems to be silent about it, and even the early Fathers of the Church say nothing about it?" Some Evangelical Protestants claim that Catholic belief in the Assumption is just the product of popular "sentiment" and "myth." So is this a doctrine that Catholics have to accept with blind faith, just because the Church says so?

Well, we can trust that in discerning such things and defining doctrine, the Church is guided by the Holy Spirit, for in 1 Timothy 3:15, St. Paul calls the Church "the pillar and bulwark of the truth." You can certainly trust a "pillar and bulwark"!

Still, it is perfectly legitimate to ask what evidence the Church had in hand when she first sought to discern the truth about this matter — and whether that evidence can stand up under scrutiny today. Besides, it is good for Catholics to explore the reasons behind this doctrine, in case we are ever asked by one of our non-Catholic friends or acquaintances why the Church believes such a thing. Remember the exhortation of St. Peter: "Always be prepared to make a defense to anyone who calls you to account for the hope that is in you" (1 Pet 3:15).

A Deafening Silence

Although it is true that the earliest Fathers of the Church do not explicitly mention the Assumption of Mary, there is an ancient and curious silence about her bodily remains that cries out for an explanation. Karl Keating of Catholic Answers writes:

> We know that after the crucifixion Mary was cared for by the apostle John (Jn 19:26-27). Early Christian writings say John went to live at Ephesus and that Mary accompanied him. There is some dispute about where she ended her life, perhaps there, perhaps back at Jerusalem. Neither of these cities nor any other claimed her remains, although there are claims about possessing her (temporary) tomb. Why did no city claim the bones of Mary? Apparently because there were no bones to claim, and people knew it.
>
> Remember, in the early Christian centuries, relics of saints were jealously guarded and highly prized. The bones of those martyred in the Colosseum, for instance, were quickly gathered up and preserved; there are many accounts of this in the biographies of those who gave up their lives for the Faith [for example, the bones of St. Peter and St. Paul were widely known to be preserved in Rome, and the sepulcher of David and the tomb of St. John the Baptist are both mentioned in Scripture; see Acts 2:29 and Mk 6:29]. Yet here was Mary, certainly the most privileged of all the saints ... but we have no record of her bodily remains being venerated anywhere.[35]

Of course, it could be argued that her remains were not pre-served and venerated by the early Christians because Mary herself was not held in special honor at that time. But we have already seen how the early Fathers of the Church exalted her as the New Eve and Mother of God, and we know from the many paintings of Mary on the walls of the catacombs in Rome, dating back to the beginning of the second century A.D., that Mary was held in veneration as far back as we can trace. Besides, Mary herself prophesied in the New Testament: "for behold, henceforth *all generations* will call me blessed" (Lk 1:48). Unless she was a false prophet, she must have been held to be specially "blessed" by every generation of Christians, including her own.

The Witness of the Early Church

Explicit mention of the Assumption of Mary begins to appear in highly embellished legendary accounts in the fourth century. We have a slightly more sober account of the event given by St. John Damascene in a copy of a letter he preserved from a fifth-century patriarch of Jerusalem named Juvenalius to the Byzantine Empress Pulcheria. The Empress had apparently asked for relics of the most Holy Virgin Mary. Patriarch Juvenalius replied that, in accordance with ancient tradition, the body of the Mother of God had been taken to Heaven upon her death, and he expressed surprise that the Empress was unaware of this fact (implying that it must have been more or less common knowledge in the Church at the time).

Patriarch Juvenalius joined to this letter an account of how the apostles had been assembled in miraculous fashion for the burial of the Mother of God, and how, after the arrival of the Apostle St. Thomas, her tomb had been opened, and her body was not there, and how it had been revealed to the apostles that she had been taken to Heaven, body and soul.

Regarding these early, somewhat legendary accounts of the Assumption, the best scholarship tends to support the summary statement of the Anglican historian H.S. Box:

> Of the early stories of the Assumption it may be said
> that all sought to supply the known fact with unknown

details. The faithful believed that Mary is body and soul in glory. Writers set to work to guess the rest of the story.[36]

Among the early Fathers of the Church, the great theologian St. Epiphanius in the fourth century clearly expressed belief in Mary's Assumption:

> Like the bodies of the saints, [Mary] has been held in honor for her character and her understanding. And if I should say anything more in her praise, she is like Elijah, who was a virgin from his mother's womb, always remained so, and was taken up, but has not seen death.[37]

In the same work, he also states that no one knows whether Mary actually died before being taken to Heaven — although "her holy body, by which light rose on the world" now rests "amid blessings."[38]

Later, in the sixth century, belief in the Assumption was defended at length by St. Gregory of Tours, and it is important to note that no saint or Father of the Church ever disputed the doctrine.

Obviously, these bits of evidence (that is, the early and deafening silence about the bones of Mary, and widespread belief in the Assumption manifest among the early Christians of the fourth and fifth centuries, without any dispute over the doctrine among the saints and the Fathers), all by themselves, do not prove conclusively that the Assumption of Our Lady really happened. But the Church believes that because of the outpouring of the Holy Spirit at Pentecost, the People of God as a whole possess what St. Augustine and St. Thomas Aquinas called an *affectio* or *inclinatio fidei*: in other words, an affective inclination, a movement of the heart that draws them to the truths of the faith. Given that the Holy Spirit is the Spirit of Truth (see Jn 16:13), a consensus of the faithful on a matter of divine truth, and especially a consensus of the saints (who are full to overflowing with the Holy Spirit), certainly must be taken as a sign of the work of the Holy Spirit, leading God's people to unfold and appreciate, more and more, the mysteries of divine revelation.

The Bible Unfolds the Truth About Mary's Assumption

Our Protestant Evangelical brothers and sisters claim that there is no mention of the Assumption of Mary in Scripture. Catholic biblical scholars such as Scott Hahn, however, argue that there is indeed an allusion to the mystery of the Assumption right in the very place we would most expect to find it if the doctrine were true: namely, in the writings of the Apostle St. John, the one into whose care our Lord placed His mother at the hour of His Death on the Cross (see Jn 19:25-27). Moreover, it occurs in what may be the last of the New Testament books to be written, a book almost certainly written after Mary's earthly life was over: the Book of Revelation.

Before looking at this passage from Revelation, however, we need to consider some important background information from the Gospel according to St. Luke. In his work *Hail, Holy Queen*, Scott Hahn shows conclusively that the story of the visitation of Mary to her cousin Elizabeth, recounted in the first chapter of St. Luke's Gospel, bears numerous and remarkable similarities to the Old Testament's account in 2 Samuel 6:1-19 of King David bringing the Ark of the Covenant up to Jerusalem:

> Down through the centuries scholars have marveled at the way Luke's gospel subtly parallels key texts of the Old Testament. One of the early examples in his narrative is the story of Mary's visitation to Elizabeth. Luke's language seems to echo the account, in the second book of Samuel, of David's travels as he brought the Ark of the Covenant to Jerusalem. The story begins as David "arose and went" (2 Sam 6:2). Luke's account of the visitation begins with the same words: Mary "arose and went" (1:39). In their journeys, then, both Mary and David proceeded to the hill country of Judah. David acknowledges his unworthiness with the words "How can the ark of the

Lord come to me?" (2 Sam 6:9) — words we find echoed as Mary approaches her kinswoman Elizabeth: "Why is this granted to me, that the mother of my Lord should come to me?" (Lk 1:43). Note here that the sentence is almost verbatim except that "ark" is replaced by "mother." We read further that David "danced" for joy in the presence of the ark (2 Sam 6:14, 16), and we find a similar expression used to describe the leaping of the child within Elizabeth's womb as Mary approached (Lk 1:44). Finally, the ark remained in the hill country for three months (2 Sam 6:11), the same amount of time Mary spent with Elizabeth.[39]

In fact, the *Ignatius Catholic Study Bible* adds another point of similarity between Luke 1 and the Old Testament stories about the Ark of the Covenant:

[Luke] brings into his story a highly significant expression once connected with the Ark. The term shows up in Lk 1:42, where Elizabeth bursts out with an exuberant cry at the arrival of Mary and her Child. Although the Greek verb translated as "exclaimed" [in the RSV] seems ordinary enough, it is hardly ever used in the Bible. In fact, it is found only here in the New Testament. Its presence in the Greek Old Testament is likewise sparse, appearing only five times. Why is this important? Because every time the expression is used in the Old Testament, it forms part of stories surrounding the Ark of the Covenant. In particular, it refers to the melodic sounds made by the Levitical singers and musicians when they glorify the Lord in song. It thus describes the "exulting" voice of the instruments that were played before the Ark as David carried it in procession to Jerusalem (1 Chr 15:28; 16:4-5), and as Solomon transferred the Ark to its final resting place in the Temple (2 Chr 5:13). Alluding to these episodes, Luke connects this same expression with the melodic cry of another Levitical descendant, the aged Elizabeth (Lk 1:5). She too lifts up her voice in liturgical praise, not before the golden chest, but before Mary. Luke's remarkable familiarity with these ancient stories enables him to select even a single word that will whisper to his readers that this young Mother of the Messiah is the new Ark of the Covenant.[40]

In short, the connections are too many to be accidental: Saint Luke means to tell us, in his own characteristic way, that Mary herself is the new Ark of the Covenant. Just as the Ark in ancient Israel contained signs of the Old Covenant — the tables of the Law, the priestly rod of Aaron, and some of the manna-bread from Heaven — so Mary's womb contained the signs of the New Covenant: the true Teacher of God's Law, the true High Priest, and the true Bread of Life, Jesus Christ the Savior. Thus, it was already a belief of the Apostolic Church that Mary — and especially her body — was the new Ark of the Covenant.

The old Ark of the Covenant had been lost for many centuries, and none of the Jews knew where it could be found. (Indeed, it remains missing to this very day.) With that in mind, let's look now at what we find at the end of chapter 11 of the Book of Revelation:

> Then God's temple in heaven was opened, and the ark of his covenant was seen within his temple, and there were flashes of lightening, voices, peals of thunder, an earthquake and heavy hail.

What an audio-visual spectacular! The Ark had been found! But look what Revelation tells us next (and remember: The chapter and verse divisions of the books of the Bible are not part of the original texts; they were inserted centuries later by monks to help us locate Scripture verses more easily, so the following sentence from the start of chapter 12 came directly after the one at the end of chapter 11 in the original manuscripts):

> And a great portent appeared in heaven, a woman clothed with the sun, with the moon under her feet, and on her head a crown of twelve stars; she was with

child. ... She brought forth a male child, one who is to
rule all the nations with a rod of iron (12:1, 5).

Clearly, what St. John was shown in his vision, recorded
here in the Book of Revelation, is that the Ark of the Covenant is
now in Heaven as a "woman clothed with the sun" whose child
is the Messiah (the one who will rule with a "rod of iron;" see
Ps 2:9). That this woman is *bodily* present in Heaven is also clear
from the fact that she is said to have the moon "under her feet"
and "on her head a crown of twelve stars" (12:1). This is in stark
contrast to the way the departed are normally referred to in the
New Testament, which elsewhere speaks of "the *souls* who had
been slain" (Rev 6:9) and "the *spirits* of just men made perfect"
(Heb 12:23).

This passage from Revelation also manifests a parallel with
the story in St. John's Gospel of Mary at the foot of the Cross.
As Catholic biblical scholar Edward Sri points out: "The woman
in Revelation 12 is the mother not only of the individual Messiah
(Rev 12:5), but also of Christians who 'keep the commandments
of God and bear testimony to Jesus' (Rev 12:17); whereas Mary
at the cross is presented not only as Jesus's mother (Jn 19:25-
26), but also as the mother of the beloved disciple — a figure
who represents all faithful disciples."[41] [NB: We will return to
this point later in Chapter Eight.] Here is another indication that
the woman of Revelation 12 is meant to be the mother of Jesus.

Indeed, several of the early Church Fathers saw this passage
in the Book of Revelation as a reference to Mary, the Mother
of our Savior, including St. Ephrem of Syria, St. Epiphanius of
Salamis, St. Ambrose, and St. Augustine.[42] The other two main
characters in Revelation 12 (the dragon and the child) clearly
represent individuals (namely, Satan and Jesus), so it is likely that
the "woman clothed with the sun" also represents an historical
individual: namely Mary, the Mother of the Messiah (see Rev
12:5) and Ark of the New Covenant.

At the same time, many of the ancient Church Fathers
saw the "woman" as a symbol of Israel, and as a symbol of the
Church, the New Israel. There are certainly indications in the text
that this is also what this "woman" symbolizes. (For instance,

she has a crown of 12 stars on her head, symbolizing the 12 tribes of Israel and the 12 apostles.) Her birth pangs may allude to the sufferings of the Daughter of Zion, the faithful Jewish people, in the run-up to the coming of the Messiah (see Is 26:17; 66:7-8). Moreover, when the "woman" flees into the desert and is protected and nourished by God after the Messiah has been enthroned in Heaven (see Rev 12:13-16), the events probably serve to illustrate how God looks after His people, the Church, after the Ascension of Christ.

So which interpretation of Revelation 12 is correct?

All three can be correct — and the Fathers saw no contradiction between them. It was not uncommon in ancient Jewish literature to employ a multiple-symbol, such as an historical individual used to symbolize a whole group of people. For example, it is quite likely that the famous passage in Isaiah 53 about the sufferings of the Messiah ("He was despised and rejected of men, a man of sorrows and acquainted with grief," etc.) was also meant to symbolize the vocation of suffering of the whole people of Israel. Similarly, in Psalm 44:4, "Jacob" stands for all of Israel, and in Rom 5:19, "Adam" represents all of humanity.

In a comparable way, Mary, the Mother of the Church, is used in Revelation to symbolize the fulfillment of the vocation of Israel in the new People of God. We are to be Christ-bearers as she was, bearing the Savior in our hearts in our mission to the world. As Edward Sri once wrote: "Mary is just the right person to embody both the Old and New Covenant People, since she herself stands at the hinge between the Old and the New. If there was one woman in history who could represent both Old Covenant Israel and the beginning of the New Covenant People of God, it would be Mary."[43] Pope Benedict XVI summed it up for us in his meditations on "John, the Seer of Patmos" in his General Audience of August 23, 2006:

> The woman represents Mary the Mother of the Redeemer, but at the same time she also represents the whole Church, the people of God of all times, the Church which in all ages, with great suffering, brings forth Christ ever anew. And she is always threatened by the dragon's power.

It is no wonder, therefore, that when the Church began to put together liturgical texts for the Feast of the Assumption, she made a connection (first made by several of the ancient Fathers) between Psalm 132:8 and the mystery of the heavenly woman-Ark: "Arise, O Lord, and go to Thy resting place, Thou and the ark of Thy might." The early Christians definitely believed that Psalm 132 was a psalm that prophesied the coming of the Messiah (for instance, see Acts 2:30). It only stands to reason, therefore, that Psalm 132:8 came to be understood by the early Fathers to mean that after the Lord "arose" from the dead, He took with Him into heavenly glory the true "Ark" of the New Covenant, the body and soul of His mother Mary. In fact, the ancient Israelites believed that the original Ark was made from incorruptible wood, so implicitly this passage also foreshadows the bodily incorruption given to Mary by Her Risen Son.

If we want further corroboration that the "woman, clothed with the sun" of Revelation 12 was meant to be a symbol of the Blessed Virgin Mary in heavenly glory, we need only look at the image of Our Lady of Guadalupe, given miraculously by Our Lady to St. Juan Diego in the 16th century (see Chapter Eleven), and compare it with the description in the Book of Revelation. Catholics can be confident that Our Lady of Guadalupe and the "woman" of Revelation 12 are one and the same person.

Evangelical Protestant writers sometimes point to John 3:13 as a decisive biblical text against the doctrine of Mary's Assumption. Jesus said: "No one has ascended into heaven, but he who descended from heaven, the Son of man." But this passage really does not apply to Mary's case at all. First, Jesus spoke these words while He was still alive — probably decades before Mary was taken into Heaven. Besides, as Tim Staples pointed out:

> The key word here would be the word *ascended*. Mary did not ascend; she was *assumed*. Jesus ascended by his own divine power as he prophesied he would in John 2:19-21 ... Mary was powerless to raise herself; she had to be assumed into heaven.[44]

In his proclamation of the doctrine of the Assumption in 1950, Pope Pius XII also noted how the Book of Genesis foreshadows Mary as intimately sharing in the same total victory of her Son over Satan: "I will put enmity between you and the woman, and between your seed and her seed" (Gen 3:15). Mark Miravalle explains:

> According to St. Paul (cf. Rom 5-8; Heb 2), the consequences of Satan's seed, evil, are twofold: sin and death (which specifically refers to bodily corruption). Therefore the Mother of Jesus, who shared in her son's victory over Satan and his seed, would also have to be saved from the two consequences of sin and death (bodily corruption). She did triumph over sin in her Immaculate Conception, and triumphed over death (corruption of the body) in her glorious Assumption at the end of her earthly life.[45]

Implicit references to the bodily assumption of great saints of the Old Testament such as Moses, Elijah, and Enoch, can be found elsewhere in the Bible (see 2 Kgs 2:10-12; Mt 27:52-53; Mk 9:2-6; Heb 11:5-6). Although none of these "assumptions" has ever been explicitly defined by the Church as an article of faith, still, the possibility of bodily triumph over death in general, and the reality of the Assumption of Mary in particular, are evidently in accord with Holy Scripture.

The Assumption and the Analogy of Faith

But even all that we have said so far about the roots of the doctrine of the Assumption in Scripture and ancient Tradition was not enough to lead the Church to definitively declare that it was a truth revealed by God. Something more was needed: what theologians call *the analogy of faith*. This means that every authentic doctrine revealed by God must be seen to "fit" with every other revealed doctrine. In other words, there must be a harmony among the truths of the Faith — and certainly no contradictions between them.

Does the doctrine of Mary's Assumption fit with the Catholic faith as a whole?

Of course it does.

First of all, it is entirely fitting that the Son of God, who loved His mother with a greater tenderness than any other son ever loved any other mother, would preserve her from the bodily corruption involved in death. As the Lord of life and death (see Rev 1:17-18), the Risen and Ascended Christ certainly had the power to do this, and therefore it is not surprising that we find evidence from Scripture and Tradition that He did.[46]

Second, the doctrine of Mary's Assumption is a natural fit with the doctrine of her Immaculate Conception: that she was preserved from the inheritance of original sin by the merits of her Son's Passion. Remember, God can do that kind of thing simply because He has all of time present to Him at once. For example, He took the merits of His Son's Passion and applied them to the patriarchs and prophets of Israel, granting them many graces on that basis. And in the same way, He took the merits of His Son's Passion, and on that basis gave to Mary an outpouring of grace in her soul from the first moment of her existence, to prepare her for her special role as Mother of the Savior.

Now, we know from the Book of Genesis that one of the results of the Fall of Adam and Eve was that all their descendants became subject to suffering and death. "The wages of sin is death" (Rom 6:23). But Mary did not share in this fallen condition. Rather, her soul was enriched from the moment of her conception with the grace of the life-giving Holy Spirit. Blessed John Henry Newman wrote: "Why should she share the curse of Adam, who had no share in his fall?" Thus, our belief in the graced origin of Mary naturally leads us to accept the truth that she was preserved from the curse and indignity of the bodily corruption involved in human death. That is why it was not until the 20th century that the Church became so sure of the doctrine of the Assumption that she proclaimed it a revealed truth from God: because it was not until the 19th century that she became convinced, beyond any reasonable doubt, of the truth of the Immaculate Conception. The one doctrine cleared the way for the other.

Most important of all, the Assumption of Mary is a loud and triumphant proclamation of *the full truth of Easter*. We sometimes say that the Easter faith, in a nutshell, is that "Christ is risen." In a certain sense, that is true enough. But the good news that the apostles proclaimed to the world was not only that Christ is risen, but that, precisely because He is risen, He is bringing His whole Mystical Body on earth to join Him one day in heavenly glory. That is what St. Peter joyfully proclaims in 1 Peter 1:3-4:

> Blessed be the God and Father of our Lord Jesus Christ! By His great mercy we have been born anew to a living hope through the resurrection of Jesus Christ from the dead, and to an inheritance which is imperishable, undefiled, and unfading, kept in heaven for you ... .

Most of the peoples of the ancient world, if they believed in life after death at all, believed merely in the immortality of the human soul: as if our ultimate goal as human beings was merely to end up as bodiless spirits like Casper the Friendly Ghost. Not much "good news" in that! The Gospel message, however, is not only that Jesus Himself rose again in a glorified body, but also that, if our hearts live in union with Him, we, too, shall rise again to a glorified life, body and soul, just like His. As St. Paul once promised: "He shall change our lowly body to be like His glorious body" (Phil 3:21). That is precisely what the Assumption of Mary proclaims: Christ is risen — and He is now bringing all faithful hearts with Him to glory. And the sign of this hope to all the Church is that the person who was closest to Christ's own loving Heart has already been raised to glory before us: *Assumpta est Maria in caelum, gaudent angeli*! ("Mary is assumed into Heaven, while angels rejoice!")

In closing, here are the words of a poem written by a young student at St. Therese Institute of Faith and Mission in Canada. It captures the wonder and the mystery of Mary's Assumption about as well as human words can possibly do:

> You're going home
> Clad in the sun, stars overhead, moon underfoot, and
>   snake under heel
> Most pure, most humble, most holy
> My mother, the well of your soul, deepened by suffering,
> But the hem of the scarlet robe did not dare touch your
>   ivory skin

Preserved from sin, but not from pain
An elegant vase, a masterpiece, a rose
Petals chosen to be preserved for all eternity
You lived and loved, then fell into sleep
Darkness danced with you, but not for long
You're going home
For from heaven reached down your beloved
The one who had your heart from the beginning
The Lord, the almighty, the alpha and omega
Comes to gather his little girl
And you re-echo your words, as you've done so
    many times before
Though dormant and still, your heart says "yes"
And you are lifted, high there
Up into the throne of his heart
The one whom you love
You're going home
He gathers up your life like roses
Every minute, he adds to the bouquet
Moments spent with his son in the sanctuary
    of your home
Kneading, sewing, talking
Moments spent on the hill where he hung
Weeping, mourning, trusting
Moments spent and gathered
In the temple, on the donkey, in the stable,
    at the wedding
Watching him take the first of his steps
And walking beside him as he takes his last
Tending his wounds, teaching him prayers
Watching him fall, calling his name
Like lilies, your beloved gathers these moments
And fashions, out of them, a new crown
One for you to wear for all eternity
So take your crown, dear mother, be not afraid
You're going home.

Janaya Trudel

PRAYER

Mary, Queen Assumed into Heaven, I rejoice that you were taken to the throne prepared for you in Heaven by the Holy Trinity.

Lift my heart with you in the glory of your Assumption … Make me realize that death is the triumphant gate through which I shall pass to your Son, and that some-day my body shall rejoin my soul in the unending bliss of Heaven.

From this earth over which I tread as a pilgrim, I look to you for help … (Mention your request).

When the hour of my death has come, lead me safely to the presence of Jesus to enjoy the vision of my God for all eternity, together with you.

(Adapted from a prayer by Fr. Lawrence Lovasik, SVD.)

QUESTIONS FOR DISCUSSION

1. What does the Bible say about the Assumption of Mary? Where is it at least implicit in the New Testament?

2. What difference does it make whether or not we believe in the Assumption of Mary? Does it add to our appreciation of the doctrine of the Immaculate Conception? Does it increase our joy in the message of Easter? Does it make Our Lady in Heaven seem closer to us?

3. Why do you think that many Protestant Christians reject the doctrine of the Assumption of Mary?

SUGGESTIONS FOR FURTHER READING

• Father Donald Calloway, MIC, Under the Mantle, the section entitled "The Blessings of Motherhood," pp. 266-273

CHAPTER SEVEN

Mary,
Queen
of Heaven

Hail, Holy Queen, Mother of Mercy.
Our life, our sweetness, and our hope ...

For many centuries, Catholics all over the world have rejoiced to honor Mary and called upon her under the title "Queen of Heaven." According to St. John's vision in Revelation 12:1, she appeared in Heaven wearing a crown of 12 stars on her head, symbolic of the 12 tribes of Israel and the 12 apostles who were the foundation stones of the New Israel, the Church. Mary is clearly the heavenly Queen of the People of God.

This title for Mary was also foreshadowed in the story of the Annunciation. When the angel Gabriel appeared to Mary, he promised her that her Son would reign forever as the Messiah:

> He will be great, and will be called the Son of the Most High, and the Lord God will give to him the throne of his father David, and he will reign over the house of Jacob forever, and of his kingdom there will be no end (Lk 1:32-33).

Now, if Mary's Son was to inherit an everlasting Kingdom, this implies that Mary was literally to be the "Queen Mother" of His Kingdom, for we know for a fact that in ancient Israel, the mother of a king usually received the role and title of "Queen Mother." As Catholic theologian Mark Miravalle points out:

> Because the kings of Israel normally had numerous wives, the mother of the king was chosen to be queen of the kingdom, due to her singular familial relationship with the king. The "Gebirah" or "Lady" of the kingdom assisted the king in the ruling of the kingdom in her noble office as the queen mother (cf. 2 Kings 11:3, 1 Kings 2:19; 1 Kings 15:9-13; Jer 13:18-20).
>
> The office and authority of the queen mother in her close relationship with the king made her the strongest "advocate" to the king for the people of the kingdom. No one had more intercessory power with the king than the queen mother, who at times

sat enthroned at the right side of the king (cf. 1 Kings 2:19-20). The queen mother also had the function of "counselor" to the king in regards to matters of the kingdom (Prov 31:8-9; 2 Chr 22:2-4). ... The Old Testament image and role of the queen mother, the "great lady," as advocate to the king for the people of the kingdom prophetically foreshadows the role of the great Queen Mother and Lady of the New Testament. For it is Mary of Nazareth who becomes Queen and Mother in the Kingdom of God, as the Mother of Christ, King of All Nations.[47]

Mary, Advocate and Mediatrix

If Mary has been exalted by God's grace to the role of Queen of Heaven, then this has tremendous implications for her relationship with the whole People of God. Let's go back again to the days of the early Christians and see the central role she played in their lives as heavenly Queen Mother of the Church. Mark Miravalle writes:

> The first historic indications of the existing veneration of Mary carried on from the Apostolic Church is manifested in the Roman catacombs. As early as the end of the first century to the first half of the second century, Mary is depicted in frescoes in the Roman catacombs both with and without her divine Son. Mary is depicted as a model of virginity with her Son; at the Annunciation; at the adoration of the Magi; and as the "orans" ("the praying one"), the woman of prayer.
>
> A very significant fresco found in the catacombs of St. Agnes depicts Mary situated between St. Peter and St. Paul with her arms outstretched to both. This fresco reflects, in the language of Christian frescoes, the earliest symbol of Mary as "Mother of the Church." Whenever St. Peter and St. Paul are shown together, it is symbolic of the one Church of Christ, a Church of authority and evangelization, a Church

for both Jew and Gentile. Mary's prominent position between Sts. Peter and Paul illustrates the recognition by the Apostolic Church of the maternal centrality of the Savior's Mother in his young Church.[48]

It is easy to appreciate what was happening here: Mary was evidently seen by the early Christians as Mother of the Church, and the Church on earth is the beginning of the Kingdom of God (see Mt 13:1-52, 16:17-19; Lk 12:32). As *Gebirah* of this Kingdom, both on earth and in Heaven, she fulfills her maternal role by acting as loving intercessor with her Son for all the needs of the People of God (with the People of God represented in the fresco by the two figures of Peter and Paul).

For these reasons, drawn both from Scripture and early Tradition, Catholics down through the ages have referred to Mary as their heavenly Queen, "Advocate" for the people of God, and even as "Mediatrix" of all the graces that Christ pours out upon the world. A mediator is someone who stands between two parties in order to help unite them — and "mediatrix" is just the word used for a female mediator.

The title "Mediatrix" was used for Mary at the Second Vatican Council, too, but the Church has not yet solemnly defined that she is Mediatrix of *all* graces. Nevertheless, this doctrine is strongly attested in the Catholic Tradition. It has been taught by numerous saints, including St. Ephrem the Syrian, St. Germanus of Constantinople, St. Bernard of Clairvaux, St. Bonaventure, St. Bernardine of Siena, St. Alphonsus Liguori, St. Louis de Montfort, and St. Maximillian Kolbe.

The logic is simple: Jesus is the source of all saving grace, and He came into the world through Mary's faithful "yes" to the angel Gabriel. She was therefore the vessel, the Mediatrix chosen by God to bring His saving grace to all mankind.

Also, as Mary participated in a unique way in the *reception* of grace by the world, it is only fitting that she participates in a unique way in the *distribution* of saving grace throughout the world. Again, we see this foreshadowed at the Annunciation, when she was implicitly named the Queen Mother of the Messianic Kingdom of her Son, and as we have seen, one of the roles of a Queen Mother was to be an advocate for the needs of the people to the king. Her role as Mediatrix was also foreshadowed in the story of the Wedding Feast at Cana, the story of the first miracle that Jesus performed to inaugurate His public ministry, a ministry that would ultimately lead to His saving death on the Cross (His "hour," as Jesus called it; see Jn 2:4). This miracle at Cana happened in response to Mary's personal mediation and intercession with Jesus on behalf of the wedding couple ("They have no more wine," Jn 2:3-5). In this way, it was Mary's intercession that actually initiated Christ's public ministry. Later, at the very end of His public ministry, Mary stood at the foot of the Cross, where her Son gave her to all the beloved disciples of Christ as their spiritual mother (see Jn 19:26-27). After the Death, Resurrection, and Ascension of Jesus, the Book of Acts tells us that the disciples were waiting and praying for nine days for the promised gift of the Holy Spirit, the one gift that could empower them for carrying out their mission. Who was there with them at the praying heart of the Church? — Mary, Mother of the Messiah, Queen Mother and Advocate for His People (see Acts 1:14). So Mary's intercession was involved in bringing about the very birth of the Church at Pentecost. In short, at every major step of Christ's mission — at the Annunciation, at Cana, on Calvary, and at Pentecost — Mary was present in faithful prayer, co-operating with divine grace and interceding for the saving work of her Son so that its benefits might be poured out upon the People of God.

Again, all of this was according to God's sovereign will. He did not *have* to arrange His plan of salvation this way: No doubt He could have accomplished His saving work in another way that did not involve the consent and cooperation of an earthly mother. And no doubt He can hear our prayers today without the added support of an intercessory mediatrix. But God wanted to associate His creatures — and especially His highest creature, Mary "full of grace" — in the saving and sanctifying work of His Son.

The saints of the Church have always been struck with awe and wonder at this special role in God's plan given to Mary, our Queen Mother, Advocate, and Mediatrix. For example, St. Ephrem the Syrian (d. 373) once wrote, "After the Mediator [Jesus Christ], you [Mary] are Mediatrix of the whole world," and St. Bernard of Clairvaux (d. 1153) was especially devoted to this title for Mary, calling her the "aqueduct" of all the graces that flow to us from Jesus Christ, insisting, "It is the will of God that we should have nothing which has not passed through the hands of Mary." Saint Bernard noted that the angel Gabriel came to deliver his message to one who was already "full of grace," and yet the angel declared that the Holy Spirit would come upon her again (see Lk 1:35): "To what purpose if it be not to fill her to overflowing? To what purpose, I repeat, except that, being filled in herself by His first coming, she might be made to superabound and overflow unto us by the second?"[49] Saint Maximillian Kolbe, the martyr of Auschwitz (d. 1941), taught that divine grace flows to the world from the Father through His Son, in the Holy Spirit, and through the intercession of Mary, who was full to overflowing with the same Holy Spirit.

Saint John Paul II called attention to another aspect of Mary's "Queenship" in his *Letter to Women* (section 10). Her reign, he said, is not one of earthly splendor and worldly power, but one of service and of love:

> Putting herself at God's service, she also put herself at the service of others: *a service of love*. Precisely through this service Mary was able to experience in her life a mysterious but authentic "reign." It is not by chance that she is invoked as "Queen of heaven and earth." The entire community of believers thus invokes her; many nations and peoples call upon her as their "Queen." *For her, "to reign" is to serve! Her service is "to reign"!*

Mary's Queenship:
Misunderstandings and Objections

Sadly, Mary's role as Queen of Heaven, Advocate, and Mediatrix of All Graces has sometimes been badly misunderstood. Our Protestant Evangelical brothers and sisters, for example, worry that this teaching violates the clear words of Scripture that there is only one Mediator with the Father, Jesus Christ His Son, on the basis of the precious Blood He shed for us on the Cross.

Saint John Paul II directly responded to this concern in his Wednesday Audience address of October 1, 1997:

> In proclaiming Christ the one mediator (cf. 1 Tim 2:5-6), the text of St. Paul's Letter to Timothy excludes any other parallel mediation, *but not subordinate mediation*. In fact, before emphasizing the one exclusive mediation of Christ, the author urges "that supplications, prayers, intercessions and thanksgivings be made for all men" (2:1). Are not prayers a form of mediation? Indeed, according to St. Paul the unique mediation of Christ is meant to encourage other, dependent, ministerial forms of mediation.[50]

What St. John Paul II and St. Paul are telling us, therefore, is that *all* Christians are called to "mediate" the grace of Christ to one another: for example, through prayer for one another, and through witnessing to the Gospel in word and deed. Our role as mediators, however, is entirely dependent upon the grace of Christ, the unique and supreme Mediator, and is intended to lead people closer to Him. The same is true for Mary: By her unique cooperation in her Son's saving work, by her example of faithful discipleship, and by her prayers, she conveys the saving grace of Christ to all her children. Indeed, she mediates grace in these ways to all of humanity, especially to all whose hearts are open to the workings of divine grace.

Moreover, the Greek word used for "one" that St. Paul used here in 1 Timothy 2:5-6 (in the phrase "one mediator") is not *monos*, which would mean "sole," but *eis*, which can mean "one" in the sense of "principal," or "first in a series." Jesus is the principal Mediator who enables many other sub-mediators to transmit the grace of God to others. Again, faithful Christians act as sub-mediators in Christ whenever they pray for their neighbors, share the Gospel with the lost, and serve the suffering and the oppressed. The merciful love of Christ thereby passes from Jesus Christ *through* His faithful disciples to those in need.

This was also the clear and explicit teaching of the Second Vatican Council in the conciliar document *Lumen Gentium* (*Light of the Nations*, 62):

For no creature could ever be counted as equal with the Incarnate Word and Redeemer. Just as the priesthood of Christ is shared in various ways both by the ministers and by the faithful, and as the one goodness of God is really communicated in different ways to His creatures, so also the unique mediation of the Redeemer does not exclude but rather gives rise to a manifold cooperation which is but a sharing in this one source.

Many Protestant Christians argue that there is no explicit indication in Scripture that we can pray to Mary as Queen, Advocate, or Mediatrix, or to any of the saints and angels in Heaven. In Scripture, prayers are always addressed to God alone. The practice of addressing prayers to other heavenly beings, it is argued, must have been borrowed from the pagans of the Roman Empire, who addressed prayers to gods and goddesses of all kinds.

Catholics cannot agree. There are several indications right in the New Testament itself that the saints in Heaven know of our struggles and prayers on earth, and join their powerful intercessory prayers to our own. Hebrews 12:1 says, "Seeing we are surrounded by so great a cloud of witnesses [that is, by all the heroes and martyrs of the faith mentioned in chapter 11], let us run with perseverance the race that is set before us." So the early Christians believed that the martyrs and heroes of faith from the past are a good example for us, and they surround us like a crowd cheering for the runners at an Olympic race. James 5:16 tells us that "the prayer of a good man has powerful effects," and gives as an example the powerful intercessions of the prophet Elijah. This reminds us that the most powerful intercessors in the Church are those most advanced in holiness. In Revelation 5:8 and 8:3-4 we are told that, in Heaven, the elders and the angels offer up the prayers of the saints (on earth) as incense before the throne of God. This implies that the angels and the elders (that is, holy Christian leaders of the past) know of our prayers on earth and join their prayers with ours now.

Put the implications of these Scripture passages together and we can surely say that, since the angels and saints can see us in our earthly struggles, and since they care about us, and since they are powerful intercessors who can and do pray for us, we can ask them to do so even more, and will be heard. That is as far as the Bible alone can take us, but it at least establishes that the invocation of the angels and saints is consonant with Scripture.

The first surviving written record of a prayer addressed specifically to Mary is dated circa 250-300 A.D.:

> We fly to your patronage
> O holy Mother of God.
> Despise not our petitions
> in our necessities,
> but deliver us from all dangers,
> O ever glorious and blessed Virgin.

Notice here that in the middle of the third century, Mary is already referred to as "Mother of God," a title for her that will not be formally decreed by the Church for another two centuries. By the fourth century, the public invocation of the angels and saints was universally present in the life of the Church, both East and West, and there is no evidence at all of any division or dispute about this practice in the early Christian community. Many of the early Fathers were quite adamant about rejecting pagan influences on the life of the Church — why did none of them ever claim that this universal custom of invoking the angels and saints was a pagan corruption of the faith? Evidently, they did not believe it was a pagan practice at all; rather, they saw the prayer partnership of struggling Christians on earth with the angels and saints in Heaven as a clear expression of the truth that in the Kingdom of Jesus Christ, death has no dominion, and that we are one Body in Christ in His Spirit, whether we are on earth, in Heaven, or in Purgatory.

Besides, the invocation of Mary, the angels, and the saints fits very well with the wider pattern of Christian doctrine (what theologians call *the analogy of faith*, as has been discussed). The Bible says that our growth in faith and holiness is aided by the intercessions of the other members of the Body of Christ (see Eph 6:18; 1 Thess 3:11-13; 1 Tim 2:1-4), and the Church on earth and Heaven is evidently closely united (see Heb 12:22-24).

It is hard to see how asking the angels and saints to pray for us amounts to pagan idolatry, while asking one's family members and friends for their prayers is not. Both acts seem to be based on similar principles of charity and intercession. Idolatry would only occur if one believed that a saint or angel could give you something that our Lord would not (as if praying to an alternate god!). But most Catholics believe no such thing. They know that authentic prayers addressed to the angels and saints are no more than *requests made to them to pray for us to Jesus Christ*. The final address of our prayers is still the same, just as in the "Hail Mary" we say: "Holy Mary, Mother of God, pray for us sinners, now and at the hour of our death."

Some Evangelical writers are concerned that addressing Mary as "Queen of Heaven" means giving her a title that comes from an idolatrous pagan cult condemned in the Old Testament (see Jer 7:18). But, as the old saying goes, this is like comparing apples and oranges. Tim Staples gives three reasons why the worship of "the Queen of Heaven" in ancient Palestine bears no resemblance at all to how Catholics relate to Mary today:

1. Jeremiah here condemns the adoration of the Mesopotamian goddess Astarte. She is in no way related to Mary ...

2. Jeremiah condemned *offering sacrifice* to "the Queen of Heaven" [and Catholics neither worship nor offer sacrifice to Mary] ...

3. That there is a counterfeit queen does not mean there can't be an authentic one.[51]

Finally, some people worry that Catholic belief in their heavenly Queen as Mediatrix of All Graces might imply that only those who explicitly ask for Mary's intercession every time they pray will actually have their prayers heard in Heaven. Mark Miravalle responds:

> Does this mean that the graces of Jesus will not be distributed unless we pray to the Blessed Virgin? No. It does, however, express the truth that whether we call directly upon the name of Mary or not, we

nonetheless receive all graces through her actual and personally willed intercession.[52]

In short, like any good and loving mother, Mary is caring for the needs of her children in ways we do not even see, and never even asked for. Only in Heaven will we begin to appreciate how Mary's loving care follows us every step of our life as we journey onward toward the eternal Kingdom of her Son.

PRAYER

Salve Regina

Hail, Holy Queen, Mother of Mercy, our life, our sweetness and our hope! To thee do we cry, poor banished children of Eve. To thee do we send up our sighs, mourning and weeping in this valley of tears! Turn, then, O most gracious Advocate, thine eyes of mercy toward us, and after this, our exile, show unto us the blessed fruit of thy womb, Jesus. O clement, O loving, O sweet Virgin Mary.

QUESTIONS FOR DISCUSSION

1. Where is Mary's role as Queen of Heaven and Queen Mother of the Kingdom indicated in Scripture?

2. How do we know that we can ask Mary and the angels and saints to pray for us?

3. Reflect on the meaning of the prayer "Hail, Holy Queen." What does this prayer mean for you personally?

SUGGESTIONS FOR FURTHER READING

- *Catechism*, entries 963-970

- Saint Alphonsus Liguori, *The Glories of Mary*, Part One, chapter 1.1, the section entitled "How Great Should be our Confidence in Mary who is Queen of Mercy"

CHAPTER EIGHT

Mary, Mother of Mercy

What do we think of when we think of a mother? In his book *Hail, Holy Queen*, Scott Hahn outlines for us how mothers and children are literally "made for each other":

> Nature keeps mother and child so close as to be almost indistinct as individuals during the first nine months of life. Their bodies are made for each other. During pregnancy, they share the same food, blood, and oxygen. After birth, nature places the child at the mother's breast for nourishment. The newborn's eyes can see only far enough to make eye contact with Mom. The newborn's ears can clearly hear the beating of a mother's heart and the high tones of the female voice. Nature has even made a woman's skin smoother than her husband's, the better to nestle with the sensitive skin of a baby. The mother, body and soul, points beyond herself to her child.[53]

A good mother is someone who cares for us tenderly, someone we can run to whenever we are hurt or sad, and someone in whom we can always find understanding and compassion. A good mother is always ready to comfort us, to care for our needs, and to help us go on when life gets hard.

Mary Immaculate is our mother of tender compassion, a mother who understands all our sorrows because her own life was full of them. The Eucharistic Apostles of The Divine Mercy (EADM)'s first *Cenacle Formation Manual* tells us that her compassion for us is rooted in her own experience of sorrow at every step of her life journey:

> Mary's life was full of contradictions. She carried the Son of God in her womb and had many joys, but also many sorrows. Reflecting on her sorrows, we recall the prophecy of Simeon (Lk 2:34-35), the flight into Egypt (Matt 2:13-14), the loss of Jesus in the Temple (Lk 2:43-45), the meeting of Jesus and Mary on the Way of the Cross, the crucifixion (Jn 19:25-27), the

taking down of the body of Jesus from the Cross, and the burial of Jesus. Each of these must have pierced her heart like a sharp sword, and inflicted pain that only a loving mother could understand.[54]

Mary: Loving Mother of St. Faustina — and Ours, Too!

The greatest saints of the Church have always turned to the compassionate Heart of our spiritual mother in Heaven. For example, several times the Blessed Virgin spoke about her maternal tenderness to the great Apostle of Divine Mercy, St. Maria Faustina Kowalska. She told her, "*Know, my daughter, that although I was raised to the dignity of Mother of God, seven swords of pain pierced my heart*" (*Diary of Saint Maria Faustina Kowalska*, 786). On another occasion, Our Lady told her, "*I know how much you suffer, but do not be afraid. I share with you your suffering, and I shall always do so*" (*Diary*, 25). Throughout Faustina's life, Mary taught her that she, Mary, is the mother who understands our joys, our sorrows, and our true needs better than anyone.

As a result, St. Faustina placed her complete trust in Mary right from the start, a childlike trust that knew no bounds. In the early pages of her *Diary*, for example, she consecrated her whole being to Mary, entrusting her life to Mary with these words:

> O Mary, my Mother and my Lady, I offer You my soul, my body, my life and my death, and all that will follow it. I place everything in Your hands (*Diary*, 79).

Later, when she went to the Shrine of Mary in Czestochowa in Poland to pray there before the great icon of Our Lady, St. Faustina wrote:

> The Mother of God told me many things. I entrusted my perpetual vows to her. I felt that I was her child and that She was my Mother. She did not refuse any of my requests (*Diary*, 260).

Toward the end of St. Faustina's life, Mary encouraged her again to place complete childlike trust in her by speaking to her these tender words: "*My daughter, at God's command I am to be, in a special and exclusive way your Mother; but I desire that you, too, in a special way, be My child*" (*Diary*, 1414).

Saint Faustina's childlike trust in Mary was especially evident in times of great suffering. It was then above all that she placed herself in the arms of her mother Mary and entrusted herself completely to Mary's tender care and heavenly intercession. In *Diary* entry 315, for example, Faustina prayed:

> Mother of God, Your soul was plunged into a sea of bitterness; look upon Your child and teach her to suffer and to love while suffering. Fortify my soul that pain will not break it. Mother of grace, teach me to live by [the power of] God.

As her physical and spiritual sufferings increased, St. Faustina again entrusted herself to the care of the Mother of God, and found strength through meditating on Mary's own patience and courage:

> O Mary, today [probably it was Good Friday] a terrible sword has pierced Your holy soul. Except for God, no one knows of Your suffering. Your soul does not break; it is brave, because it is with Jesus. Sweet Mother, unite my soul to Jesus, because it is only then that I will be able to endure all trials and tribulations, and only in union with Jesus will my little sacrifices be pleasing to God. Sweetest Mother, continue to teach me about the interior life. May the sword of suffering never break me. O pure Virgin, pour courage into my heart and guide it (*Diary*, 915).

Whether in times of sorrow or of joy, again and again the Blessed Virgin Mary was the one St. Faustina turned to for help in living in close union with Jesus Christ. It is not surprising, therefore, that the Mother of God often appeared or spoke to St. Faustina right before Holy Communion, as if Mary's special task was to prepare Faustina for receiving Jesus in the Blessed Sacrament (for instance, *Diary*, 449, 597, 608, 846, 1414). As Faustina wrote in *Diary* entry 840:

> I am spending this time with the Mother of God, and preparing myself for the solemn moment of the coming of the Lord Jesus. The Mother of God is instructing me in the interior life of the soul with Jesus, especially in Holy Communion.

This is precisely what we should expect. Jesus says to us in the Book of Revelation (3:20): "Behold. I stand at the door and knock: if any man hears My voice and opens the door, I will come in to him, and will sup with him, and he with Me." So at each Holy Communion, Jesus stands at the door of our hearts and knocks — but He will not force His way in. As He said, He waits for us to "open the door" and let Him in of our own free will. We may think to ourselves: "Of course I will let Him in; I will welcome Him and accept Him as my Lord and Savior every day of my life, and at every Holy Communion." Sadly, however, it is not as easy as that. The door of the human heart is heavy with pride; the hinges, rusted by our doubts; the latches, chained by our fears. It is not so easy to swing such a door open, even if we want to do so. And that is another reason we have such need of Mary, our Mother of Mercy. She is always ready to help us by her prayers to open the door of our hearts to her Son.

We, too, can come to know and cherish Mary, as St. Faustina did, as our spiritual mother who intercedes for all our needs. Relating to Mary in this way was not just a special privilege given to the saints; it is open to all the People of God. Father Peter John Cameron, OP, humorously sums up this truth in his book *Mysteries of the Virgin Mary*: "Adam was the only man in history who did not have a mother. God saw what a mess it got him into and made sure that that never happened again. As a result of Adam's sin, God would save humankind, and salvation would have a mother."[55]

More Scriptural Roots

We have already seen that Scripture teaches that Mary was chosen at the Annunciation to be Queen Mother of her Son's Kingdom. As our heavenly Queen, she is Advocate for the People of God and maternal intercessor for us all as we journey toward Heaven. We saw this reflected, too, in the story of the Wedding Feast at Cana, and the cenacle of prayer at Pentecost. The Book of Revelation hints at this as well when it speaks of the heavenly "woman clothed with the sun" who gave birth to the Messiah, and of "*the rest of her offspring* ... those who keep the commandments of God and bear testimony to Jesus" (Rev 12:17). All of these Bible passages *implicitly* teach us that Mary is our spiritual mother.

The Bible also tells us that Jesus *explicitly* bestowed this role upon Mary when He was dying on the Cross. He said to her: "Woman, behold your son," and then, turning to His Beloved Disciple, St. John, "Son, behold your mother" (Jn 19:25-27). According to the ancient Fathers of the Church, all Christian believers were prefigured in this Beloved Disciple who stood beneath the Cross, and to whom Jesus said, "Behold your mother." Thus, Mary was called to be not only St. John's mother, but our mother, too, the mother of all the faithful disciples of Christ. What this means is that Christ gave her to us to be our mother in Heaven, who ever comes to our aid by her loving intercessions on our behalf. If she is willing to intercede for us and pray for us, and thereby open the door to all the graces that Christ wants to shower upon us, then she is indeed our "Mother of Mercy" — for all of God's graces are acts of His Divine Mercy to weak and sinful creatures like us. In short, by her maternal intercession and compassion for us, Mary opens the floodgates to the full outpouring of God's merciful love upon the world.

What a tremendous gift Jesus gave to every Christian from the Cross! Tim Staples explains that Mary is actually a double gift to us on our journey toward Heaven:

On the cross our Lord and Savior gifted us with two things that he knew he could never be for us: *a perfect mother* and a *perfect disciple of Christ,* in whom we can find and experience the hope that is necessary for salvation.[56]

The Second Vatican Council summed up for us the mystery of Mary as our spiritual mother and Mother of Mercy in the document *Lumen Gentium* (*Light of the Nations,* 62):

> The motherhood of Mary in the order of grace lasts without interruption from the consent which she faithfully gave at the annunciation, and which she sustained without hesitation under the cross until the eternal fulfillment of all the elect. In fact, being assumed into heaven, she has not laid aside this office of salvation, but by her manifold intercession, she continues to obtain for us the graces of eternal salvation. By her maternal charity, she takes care of the brethren of her Son who still journey on earth surrounded by dangers and difficulties, until they are led into their blessed home.

On Calvary, Mary Was Called to be Our Spiritual Mother

Our Evangelical Protestant brothers and sisters often object to the way Catholics read the story in St. John's Gospel about Mary at the foot of the Cross. They say:

> Surely, you are just reading into this Bible passage a meaning that the author never intended to convey. The Apostle John was not trying to tell us that Mary was explicitly commissioned by Jesus from the Cross to be the spiritual Mother of all Christians. Rather, John was simply showing us how Jesus lovingly made provision for the support of His Mother, so that someone would take care of her after He had gone.

Needless to say, Catholics are convinced that there is a lot more going on in this passage than that!

First of all, notice that neither Mary nor John is referred to by a proper name here. Mary is called "woman" (recalling the way Jesus spoke to her at the Wedding Feast at Cana, when she interceded for the wedding couple in John 2:1-4, and the "woman" of Genesis 3:15-16, who, as Mother of the Messiah, was prophesied to be at "enmity" with Satan, along with her Son). Saint John is called in this passage simply "the disciple whom Jesus loved." The fact that Mary and John are referred to in these symbolic ways implies that there is more going on here than just a touching story about how Jesus looked after the need of His mother for a proper roof over her head.

Second, it is doubtful that there was any need for Jesus to find someone to take care of Mary after His death. He must have left Mary in the care of relatives many years before when He first left home to begin His ministry in Galilee. Saint John Paul II pointed this out in his Wednesday Audience address of April 23, 1997:

> In departing from Nazareth to start his public life, Jesus had already left his mother alone. Moreover, the presence at the cross of her relative, Mary of Clopas, allows us to suppose that the Blessed Virgin was on good terms with her family and relatives, who could have welcomed her after her son's death.

Third, this passage regarding Mary at the foot of the Cross seems to be as much about the Beloved Disciple being entrusted to Mary's care as the other way around: "Behold your mother!" (Jn 19:27). The Gospel says that from that very hour, John "took her to his own home," which is the same Greek phrase used in another important place in John's Gospel. Catholic apologist Kenneth Howell explains:

> The phrase in Greek, *eis ta idia* [to his own] can indicate a more personalized reception, so that John's action is much deeper than physical care. It is exactly the same phrase used by John in 1:11 where he says

that Jesus "came unto his own (*eis ta idia*) but his own
did not receive him." 1:11 does not mean that Jesus
came to his own house, but that Jesus came to his very
own people, i.e., the Jews. So what does the phrase
mean in 19:27? It means that John received Mary as
his very own mother, just as Jesus commanded him.
He took her not only in a physical sense; he received
her into his heart. We are asked to do the same. As
beloved disciples of the Lord, we should also receive
Mary as our very own mother.[57]

Fourth, Jesus must have been referring to Mary's *spiritual*
motherhood in this passage because He spoke to St. John about
it when the apostle's own natural mother was standing right
next to him at the foot of the Cross (see Mt 27:55-56). Clearly,
John did not need a natural mother to care for, or to care for
him: He already had one! Mary's new relationship with him as
his "mother," therefore, had to be something quite different,
something spiritual.

Finally, St. John's Gospel tells us that Jesus' act of entrusting the Beloved Disciple and Mary to each other was the very last
thing that He needed to accomplish before His death. Saint John
Paul II explained that immediately after Jesus' words to them,
"the evangelist added a significant clause: 'Jesus, knowing that
all was now finished' (Jn 19:28), as if he wished to stress that he
had brought his sacrifice to completion by entrusting his mother
to John, and in him, to all men, whose mother she became in the
work of salvation."[58] In other words, this important, symbolic
act of entrusting all the beloved disciples of Christ into the care
of Mary, making her the spiritual mother of the faithful, brought
Christ's ministry on earth to an end just prior to the completion
of His sacrifice on the Cross. It was evidently the last thing He
needed to accomplish before His saving work on earth was done.

Saint John Paul II summed up his reflections on Mary at
the foot of the Cross with these thoughts:

Jesus' words, "Behold your son" effect what they
express, making Mary the mother of John, and of
all the disciples destined to receive the gift of divine

grace. On the cross, Jesus did not proclaim Mary's universal motherhood formally, but established a concrete maternal relationship between her and the beloved disciple. In the Lord's choice we can see his concern that this mother should not be interpreted in a vague way, but should point to Mary's intense, personal relationship with individual Christians. May each one of us, precisely through the concrete reality of Mary's universal motherhood, fully acknowledge her as our own Mother, and trustingly commend ourselves to her maternal care.[59]

In other words, the Holy Father was telling us that the motherhood of Mary in the order of grace is not just a doctrine to be defended: It is an invitation to a personal relationship with our real mother in Heaven. God has no motherless orphans in His world. As His own Son needed an earthly mother, so do we need a spiritual mother. From the Cross, Jesus shared His own mother with us, for we always need to be guided and spiritually nurtured with a mother's love. Mark Miravalle said it best in his book *Meet Your Mother*:

Jesus, being fully human, also needed his mom. I believe he needed his mom as he suffered in agony on the Cross. I believe she was for him a precious drop of consolation in the midst of an ocean of bitterness. And I further believe that he wants us to have no less a consolation than he himself had, that he wants us to have his mother as our spiritual mother.[60]

PRAYER

O sweetest and holy virgin, look down with the eyes of thy mercy on all the afflictions and all the afflicted that fill the earth. Behold the many poor people, the many widows and orphans, the sick troubled with so many diseases, the captives and the prisoners, the thousands

who are cursed and persecuted by the malice of men, the defenseless persons oppressed by the strong and the mighty, the seafarers and pilgrims struggling against perils on sea and land, the missionaries exposed to countless dangers in their task of saving endangered souls. Look down upon the number of afflicted minds, of anguished hearts, of souls tormented by manifold temptations, and of souls suffering …
[in] Purgatory. But above all, have pity on the countless souls that are in the state of sin and … groaning under the tyranny and bondage of [the Devil] …

Mother of Mercy, take pity on such great misery. Thou seest, alas, that the earth is crowded with miserable hearts enslaved by Satan, hearts that do not feel the extreme misfortune in which they are plunged! Mother of Grace, I offer thee all of these … by thy most compassionate heart, I beg thee to take pity on them. Break their chains asunder; implore thy beloved son, Who came into the world to enlighten all men, that He deign to give sight to the blind, and to remove from sinners their hearts of stone, replacing them with hearts obedient to the inspirations of the Holy Spirit.

Mother of Fair Love, I also offer thee the hearts of those of thy children who are faithful, who love and honor thee as their cherished Mother. Preserve and increase the precious treasure which is theirs, that they may love thee more and more, and become more worthy to be the true children of thy heart (St. John Eudes).

QUESTIONS FOR DISCUSSION

1. Describe the relationship that St. Faustina had with the Blessed Virgin Mary. How can we have a similar relationship with Mary as our spiritual mother today?

2. Some people have had very unhappy, broken relationships with their own earthly mothers. How can Mary help bring healing into the lives of such people?

3. How do we know what St. John intended to communicate to his readers by including in his Gospel the story of Jesus' words to Mary and John from the Cross? What clues do we have about what this Bible passage really means?

SUGGESTIONS FOR FURTHER READING

- Father Calloway's *Under the Mantle*, the section entitled "Mary Christmas," pp. 48-57, about Mary's motherhood of Jesus — and of all her spiritual children

Chapter Nine

Mary's Immaculate Heart

Whenever we speak of the human "heart," we commonly say things like "What's on your heart?" or "That really touched my heart" or "I can tell that what you wrote came straight from the heart." In all of these expressions, we are speaking of the heart as a symbol of the deepest mystery of a person: what a person, deep down, really thinks, feels, and desires. The *Catechism* tells us in entry 2563:

> The heart is our hidden center, beyond the grasp of our reason and of others; only the Spirit of God can fathom the human heart and know it fully.

When we speak of the "Heart of Jesus," therefore, we are referring to the deepest mystery of His person: the unfathomable love of the divine Son of God incarnate for His Heavenly Father, and for us. As I wrote in my book *Jesus, Mercy Incarnate*:

> According to the Bible, some people are cold-hearted or hard-hearted; they have hearts of "stone" (e.g. Ezek 11:19). The mystery of the Heart of Jesus, however, has been revealed to us through the Gospels, and beautifully expressed in His apparitions to St. Margaret Mary. Whatever we may say about other human hearts, this person, Jesus of Nazareth, has a heart that is aflame with love: love for His heavenly Father and love for us. That is why He showed His physical Heart to St. Margaret Mary as flaming with fire, surmounted by a cross, and pierced and surrounded by thorns. All of these were clear signs and symbols that *this Heart — the person of Jesus Christ — is pure love: the Sacred Heart of Jesus as all love and all lovable.*[61]

In a similar way, when we speak of the Immaculate Heart of Mary, we are pointing to the deepest mystery of her person. We are pointing to the mystery of love that finds expression in all that she said, did, and suffered. That is why the Catholic Tradition symbolically depicts the Heart of Mary as surrounded by flames, shining with light, and encircled by pure white flowers: because her deep, "hidden center" was completely pure, never stained by any sin at all (hence, we call her Heart "immaculate"). In fact, divine grace made her Heart as transparent as a clean clear-glass window, so that the fire and light of the Holy Spirit shone through her every thought, word, and deed at every moment.

What Mary's Physical Heart Signifies

The great troubadour of the Heart of Mary was St. John Eudes (1601-1680). In beautiful French prose, he never tired of singing of the wonders of her graces and virtues.

In his classic work *The Admirable Heart of Mary*, St. John Eudes distinguished between the "corporeal" and "spiritual" Heart of Mary. With regard to her corporeal or physical Heart, he listed a number of privileges that her Heart enjoyed, even when considered as a mere organ of her body:

> The *first* prerogative consists in the fact that the heart is the principle of the life of our holy Mother. It is the principle of all the functions of her bodily, maternal life, ever holy in itself and in its every function and employment. It is the source of the life of the Mother of God, the life of her who gave birth to the only Son of God, the life of the woman through whom God gave life to all the children of Adam, sunk as they were in the abyss of eternal death. Finally, her heart is the source of a life so holy, so noble, so sublime that it is more precious in the sight of God than the lives of all the angels and men.
>
> The *second* prerogative of the corporeal heart of Mary is that it produces the virginal blood with which the sacred body of the God-Man was formed in the chaste womb of the Blessed Mother.
>
> The *third* prerogative of Mary's heart of flesh is that it was the source of the human, material life of the Infant Jesus during the nine months that he dwelt in Mary's sacred womb. While the infant is

in its mother's bosom, the mother's heart is to such an extent the source of the infant's life that both the mother and the infant can be said to depend on it for their existence. Mary's admirable heart was therefore the source of the holy life of the Mother of God, and of her only son, the humanly divine as well as the divinely human life of the God-Man.[62]

Every mother can appreciate what St. John Eudes is saying here. A mother knows and feels that both she and her child totally depend upon the life-blood circulating within her at every moment. Indeed, the first sound that a child ever hears is the beating of his own mother's heart.

If such was the dignity of Mary's Heart considered merely as an organ of her body, how much greater was the dignity of what her physical Heart also signifies: the deepest mystery of her person, her immeasurable love for God and for us. Saint John Eudes puts it this way:

If the virginal heart beating in the consecrated breast of the Virgin of virgins, the most excellent organ of her holy body, is so admirable, as we have already seen, what must be the marvels of her spiritual heart? ... We have already considered the rare prerogatives of her heart of flesh, and we shall now endeavor to express the incomparable gifts and inestimable treasures with which her spiritual heart is filled ...

First of all, divine bounty miraculously preserved the heart of the Mother of our Savior from the stain of sin, which never touched it because God filled it with grace from the moment of its creation, and clothed it with purity so radiant that, next to God's, it is impossible to conceive of greater purity. His divine majesty possessed her heart so completely from its first instant that it never ceased to belong entirely to Him and to love Him more ardently than all the holiest hearts of Heaven and earth united.[63]

Mary's Heart Grew in Grace and Mercy

As we have seen in the chapter of this book on the Immaculate Conception, Mary's Heart was filled to overflowing with divine love right from the first moment of her life. However, it was still possible for her to experience an increase of grace, and an increase of the virtues of faith and love. After all, Mary was (and is) a real human being, a woman who experienced all the joys, pains, and sorrows of a fully human existence. This means that the more she surrendered in love and trust to the Holy Spirit day by day, in every circumstance, the stronger those virtues in her Heart became. While she possessed the unique, original grace of an immaculate conception, this was only the starting point of an increase of grace in her Heart throughout her life journey. In a similar way, the grace we are given in our own Baptism is only the beginning of a whole lifetime of opportunities to grow in grace (see Eph 5:18; 1 Pet 2:2-3; 2 Pet 3:18).

In his book *True Devotion to the Immaculate Heart of Mary* (2005), Fr. Robert Fox gave to the Church a clear exposition of the Blessed Virgin's journey into ever deeper holiness, and we shall quote his excellent treatment of this subject at length. He wrote:

> What is holiness? Essentially holiness is the possession of sanctifying grace. It is made present in a person from the moment of baptism, making one resemble God ... . We grow in holiness by doing the will of God once His sanctifying grace is implanted in our souls at baptism. Then everything done for the love of God makes one grow in grace. An increase of grace is achieved by every good work, every prayer, every loving act ... .
>
> God first loves us. If we respond in faith to his love, we grow in grace. That grace first given to children in baptism is entirely out of the goodness of God's heart, with no act of faith or response on their part. The same was true of Mary in an eminent way.

Mary did not merit her Immaculate Conception ... [T]his is why Mary is called God's masterpiece. He has given this woman a dignity worthy of his Mother, with more grace than all the angels and saints taken together ... .

What growth of grace took place in her at the Annunciation! ... God chose to use her Immaculate Heart to accept the Savior in freely agreeing to become the Mother of the Most High, the Word incarnate, the Messiah, the long-awaited One ... .

Mary says "Yes." The increase of grace in the soul of Mary when she answers "Yes" for the whole world is unimaginable. The fact that God in his loving providence looked to the free consent of Mary for the Word to be made flesh and dwell among us gives a Marian quality to every aspect of Christianity ... .

There was then the carrying of the Word made flesh in her holy womb for nine months. She became the world's first tabernacle for the Word Incarnate. Today in the tabernacles of our churches, He is present in the Most Blessed Sacrament ... as she carried Him under her heart she continuously grew in grace ... .

Grace grew in Mary as she nurtured the infant Jesus, tended to His growing needs, served Him at table, performed domestic duties. In a human way she taught Jesus as any good mother teaches her child ...

Mary was with Jesus to the end as He hung dying on the cross, redeeming the world. As grace was merited for the world, abundant grace flowed into her Immaculate Heart during those hours beneath the cross of redemption ...

Mary grew in grace after the Ascension of Christ by the reception of her divine incarnate Son in Holy Communion. After the redemptive acts of the Cross, the Apostle John took her into his own home (see Jn 19:27). We may be sure that our Blessed Lady received the Holy Eucharist frequently, even daily, as was the practice of the early Christians (see Acts 2:46). She lived with John the priest, the beloved disciple ... .

The Holy Spirit came upon Mary when she conceived the Christ Child. Now that the Church is to be identified as Christ's body, with the Holy Spirit as its Soul, this Spirit of Love descended upon all in the upper room and found a special temple adorned for His presence in Mary's heart ...

Such magnificent beauty, such radiant brightness of the light of life, we see in Mary's Immaculate Heart.[64]

The result of this incredible journey of growth in grace was that Mary's Heart became the source of the greatest possible joy to the Heart of Jesus. Proverbs 8:31 tells us that "The Lord's delight is in the children of men," and in the Gospels, we are taught that the Good Shepherd "rejoices" whenever He finds His lost sheep and brings them home (see Lk 15:5-7). How much greater must be His delight in the Heart of His mother, Mary, whose soul was always perfectly receptive to His grace and never failed to return love for love!

Mary's Immaculate Heart is Full of Divine Mercy

At the same time, while Mary was growing every day in sanctifying grace, and united at all times in the center of her soul with the Heart of her Son, she was also completely filled with His merciful love. Saint John Eudes tells us:

To the heart of Mary God communicated in great abundance His merciful inclinations, and established in it the throne and reign of His mercy more gloriously than the heart of any other creature, save the sacred humanity of Christ.

Divine Mercy reigns so perfectly in Mary's heart that she bears the name of Queen and Mother of Mercy. And the most loving Mary has so completely won the heart of God's mercy that He has given her the key to all His treasures, and made her absolute mistress of them. St. Bernard says, "She is called the Queen of Mercy because she opens the abyss and treasure of Divine Mercy to whom she chooses, when she chooses, and as she chooses."

Divine Mercy holds such complete sway over Mary's heart and fills it with such compassion for sinners and for all persons in need that Saint Augustine addresses her thus, "Thou art the sinner's only hope" after God. "My dearest children, " says Saint Bernard, "her heart is the ladder by which sinners go up to heaven; this is my reliance; this is the only reason of my hope."[65]

What does this mean for us today? It means that Mary's Heart is now a living fountain of divine love and sanctifying grace. She looks upon the hearts of her children as parched and arid ground, but with plenty of potential, needing only to be watered by divine grace and planted with the seeds of the Gospel in order to spring into abundant life.

In fact, there is no place in the whole created universe where we can draw closer to the Heart of Jesus than the Heart of Mary. Her Heart is the chapel where Jesus forever dwells, ready to pour out His merciful love upon us whenever we come to Him.

Let us always seek Him there, in the Heart of Mary, where we shall always surely find Him.

PRAYER

Blessed John Henry Newman's "Litany to the Immaculate Heart of Mary"

> Immaculate Heart of Mary, gentle and humble of heart
> — make our hearts like the Heart of Jesus.
> Heart of Mary — pray for us!
> Heart of Mary, united with the Heart of Jesus, …
> Heart of Mary, Temple of the Trinity, …
> Heart of Mary, home of the Incarnate Word, …

Heart of Mary, overflowing with grace, …
Heart of Mary, blessed among all hearts, …
Heart of Mary, abyss of humility, …
Heart of Mary, sacrifice of love, …
Heart of Mary, crucified, …
Heart of Mary, consolation of the afflicted, …
Heart of Mary, refuge of sinners, …
Heart of Mary, hope of the dying, …
Heart of Mary, seat of mercy, …
Heart of Mary — pray for us!
Immaculate Mary, gentle and humble of heart — make
our hearts like the Heart of Jesus.

QUESTIONS FOR DISCUSSION:

1. What does the Catholic Tradition mean by the human
   "heart" — and especially the Heart of Jesus?

2. How can we grow in grace throughout our life
   journey, as the Heart of Mary did?

3. How would you describe "the Heart of Mary" to
   someone who had never heard this phrase before?

SUGGESTIONS FOR FURTHER READING

- Father Michael Gaitley, MIC, *33 Days to Morning
  Glory* (Stockbridge: Marian Press, 2011), the section
  entitled "Week Three: St. Mother Teresa," on her
  devotion and consecration to the Hearts of Jesus
  and Mary, pp. 65-83

CHAPTER TEN

Mary, Co-Redemptrix

In recent years, there has been much debate and discussion in the Catholic world about the tradition, drawn from the writings of many saints and popes, of calling the Blessed Virgin Mary the "Co-Redemptrix" of the human race.

The issue is really not as complex as this theological term might make it sound. Let's look at how two of today's leading Catholic authors explain the matter.

First, Mark Miravalle, professor of theology at Franciscan University of Steubenville in Ohio, tells of an encounter he had had with St. Teresa of Calcutta, during which she expressed the truth of Mary's redemptive role in all its simplicity:

> Sacred Scripture profoundly reveals the role of our Blessed Mother as Co-Redemptrix. At the Annunciation, when Mary says "yes" to the angel and thereby gives her "fiat" (Lk 1:38), she gives to the Redeemer the instrument of redemption, His human body. In a discussion I had with the late Mother Teresa of Calcutta regarding the solemn papal definition of the co-redemptive role of Our Lady, within the first two minutes of speaking, Mother said, "Of course she is Co-Redemptrix, of course. She gave Jesus his body and the body of Jesus is what saved us." I replied, "Mother, that's the difference between sanctity and theology. You say in two minutes what it takes the theologians three volumes to write."[66]

Second, in an extended endnote to his book *33 Days to Morning Glory*, Fr. Michael Gaitley, MIC, clearly explained the propriety of using this title for Mary and what it can mean for us today. We have reprinted his entire explanation below:

> It is a doctrine of the Catholic Faith that we are called to participate in Jesus' redeeming action in the world. In other words ... Jesus doesn't just redeem us and then expect us to kick back and relax. On the contrary, he includes us in the work of redemption, and an important part of this work is our suffering.

Specifically, Jesus invites us to unite our suffering with his in order to save souls: He invites us to be "co-redeemers," redeemers "with Him," though in an entirely subordinate way to himself.

We approach the mystery of "co-redemption" when we reflect on some puzzling words of St. Paul: "I rejoice in my sufferings for your sake, and in my flesh I complete what is lacking in the suffering of Christ for the sake of his body, the Church" (Col 1:24). How can St. Paul write that there's something "lacking" in the suffering of Christ? Jesus' suffering is objectively enough to save everyone, and the graces of his suffering are available to all. In this sense, there's absolutely nothing lacking in his suffering. Yet there's a kind of "lack" in Christ's suffering in the sense that not everyone subjectively accepts his grace and mercy. Moreover, there's also a lack in his suffering when people don't fully accept his grace and mercy, that is, when they do so half-heartedly and with reservations and conditions. It's precisely in such situations where people reject or don't fully accept God's grace that our sufferings and prayers can come in to "complete what is lacking."

So, Jesus didn't come to take away our suffering — he came to transform it. With Christ, suffering is no longer a meaningless burden. Yes, we still suffer, but now, if we're in the state of grace and unite our sufferings to those of Jesus, they have salvific value; they save souls; they give life to others. "That's great," you might be saying, "but how do I unite my sufferings to Christ?" It's simple. Give them to Mary. Mary was most united to Jesus in his suffering on the Cross, and when we give her our sufferings, she herself unites them to those of Jesus and to her own. Yes, even to *her own.*

Mary's sufferings at the foot of the Cross were greater than the sufferings of any other creature, and she offered them with the greatest love. To better understand her suffering and love, reflect on the following: If you were to ask any mother who has a child that is suffering terribly if she would rather switch places with her child, of course, she would immediately respond that she would switch places without hesitation. Such is the love of a mother. Now, just think that if you took all the love in the heart of every mother in the cosmos and put it into one heart, that love wouldn't equal the love that Mary has for Jesus. Also, consider that her son is the most loveable of all. Now consider that he was brutally beaten, insulted, and slowly killed right in front of her. Imagine her suffering? We cannot. Hers truly is the greatest suffering of any creature. Her heart was truly pierced with a sword. She truly was "spiritually crucified" with Jesus through love, through her perfectly compassionate love.

Now, if I can be a "co-redeemer" with Christ by offering up my own puny sufferings to Him, then obviously Mary is also a co-redeemer. In fact, because of her extraordinary suffering with Christ, she deserves a special title, which many popes have given her: "Co-Redemptrix." This title doesn't mean that she's equal to Christ but rather that she suffered with him in an extraordinary and subordinate way. (The prefix "co" doesn't mean "equal to" but "with.") This title is in recognition that she, more than anyone else, cooperated in Christ's work of redemption. And just as she has a special role in the Body of Christ of giving birth to "other Christs" through her prayers, so she has a special role in uniting us to Jesus' saving death. It's her job to help us unite our sufferings with Jesus, to bring us, in our suffering, face to face with the love of the Heart of Jesus crucified. Moreover, she augments the merits of our sufferings with her unfathomable merits, merits that she won through her painful union with Christ on the Cross as his loving mother.

How good it is to be consecrated to Mary! She helps us not to waste our sufferings. She unites them, with her own, to the Cross of Christ. Thus, she makes our sufferings superabundantly meaningful and meritorious for the life of the world.[67]

Some theologians today worry that for the Church officially to declare Mary "Co-Redemptrix" — that is, to make it the fifth solemnly defined dogma about Mary (alongside the dogmas that Mary is the Mother of God, Ever Virgin, immaculately conceived, and assumed body and soul into Heaven) — could deal a death-blow to progress in ecumenical relations with our Protestant brothers and sisters (especially with the Evangelicals). No doubt there would be grave concern expressed at first, but it is not clear that in the long run this would be such a disaster to ecumenism. Mothers have a way of uniting broken families, and the family of Christ actually might draw closer together if challenged to examine more closely the love of the mother of the family of God. Besides, the Church does not have to begin with a solemn definition: It could begin the conversation instead by proclaiming a feast day dedicated to "Mary, Co-Redemptrix," or establishing a series of international congresses dedicated to pondering the mystery of Mary as Co-Redemptrix. In the end, it is the clear light of the fullness of revealed truth that will draw all Christians in the Holy Spirit together, not any stratagem of keeping silent on controversial matters in order to keep people from getting upset. Mark Miravalle and Fr. Michael Gaitley have pointed the way. Let's pray that when the time is right, the Church will proclaim the fullness of the truth about Our Lady in all its splendor!

PRAYERS

The Memorare

Remember, O most gracious Virgin Mary, that never was it known that anyone who fled to thy protection, implored thy help, or sought thine intercession was left unaided.

Inspired by this confidence, I fly unto thee, O Virgin of virgins, my mother; to thee do I come, before thee I stand, sinful and sorrowful. O Mother of the Word Incarnate, despise not my petitions, but in thy mercy hear and answer me. Amen.

The Stabat Mater

At the cross her station keeping,
Stood the mournful Mother weeping,
Close to Jesus to the last.
Through her heart, His sorrow sharing,
All His bitter anguish bearing,
Now at length the sword had pass'd.

Oh, how sad and sore distress'd
Was that Mother highly blest
Of the sole-begotten One!
Christ above in torment hangs;
She beneath beholds the pangs
Of her dying glorious Son.

Is there one who would not weep,
Whelm'd in miseries so deep
Christ's dear Mother to behold?
Can the human heart refrain
From partaking in her pain,
In that Mother's pain untold?

Bruis'd, derided, curs'd, defil'd,
She beheld her tender child
All with bloody scourges rent.
For the sins of His own nation,
Saw Him hang in desolation,
Till His spirit forth He sent.

O thou Mother! fount of love!
Touch my spirit from above;
Make my heart with thine accord.

Make me feel as thou hast felt;
Make my soul to glow and melt
With the love of Christ our Lord.

Holy Mother! pierce me through;
In my heart each wound renew
Of my Saviour crucified.
Let me share with thee His pain,
Who for all my sins was slain,
Who for me in torments died.

Let me mingle tears with thee,
Mourning Him who mourn'd for me,
All the days that I may live.
By the cross with thee to stay,
There with thee to weep and pray,
Is all I ask of thee to give.

Virgin of all virgins best,
Listen to my fond request
Let me share thy grief divine.
Let me, to my latest breath,
In my body bear the death
Of that dying Son of thine.

Wounded with His every wound,
Steep my soul till it hath swoon'd
In His very blood away.
Be to me, O Virgin, nigh,
Lest in flames I burn and die,
In His awful Judgment day.

Christ, when Thou shalt call me hence,
Be Thy Mother my defence,
Be Thy cross my victory.
While my body here decays,
May my soul Thy goodness praise,
Safe in Paradise with Thee. Amen.

QUESTIONS FOR DISCUSSION

1. According to St. Teresa of Calcutta, what did Mary give to Jesus that was a unique contribution to His saving work?

2. According to Fr. Michael Gaitley, MIC, how did Our Lady share in a special way in Christ's saving work on the Cross?

3. Following Mary's example, how can we too become "co-redeemers," with her, in union with her Son?

SUGGESTION FOR FURTHER READING

- Mark Miravalle, *"With Jesus": The Story of Mary Co-Redemptrix*. Goleta, CA: Queenship, 2003.

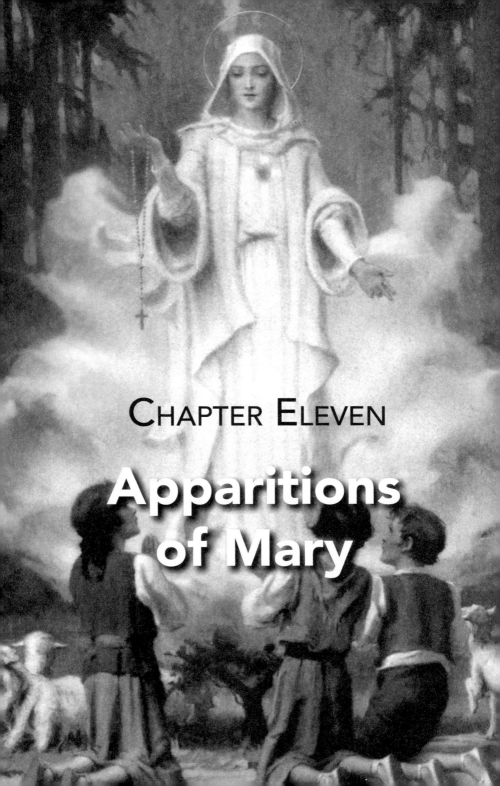

CHAPTER ELEVEN

Apparitions of Mary

Faithful Catholics not only believe in the doctrines that the Church teaches about Mary; as we have already seen in this book, we believe also that Mary is our spiritual mother in Heaven — a real person alive in Christ who prays for us, comforts us, and shows us the way to follow her Son with faith and love. This personal love of Our Lady for each and every person is the heart and soul of the Marian dimension of Catholicism, and it finds supreme expression in the way Catholics cherish the many appearances of Mary to the People of God down through history.

Why has the Blessed Virgin appeared so often — especially over the last 200 years? Consider this: Does a loving mother sit back and wait for her lost and suffering children to come home to her for help, or does she do everything she can to reach out to them when they are in trouble? In this chapter, we will look briefly at four of the greatest Marian apparitions, four dramatic interventions of Mary in the affairs of humanity, and the continuing relevance of the messages that she delivered as our spiritual mother, seeking to lead us out of the darkness and back to the light of her Son.

1. OUR LADY OF GUADALUPE, MEXICO, 1531

When the Eucharistic Apostles of The Divine Mercy (EADM), an apostolate of the Congregation of Marian Fathers of the Immaculate Conception, sought a heavenly patron for their work of evangelism and outreach, it was only natural for their founder, Dr. Bryan Thatcher, to turn to the patronage of Our Lady of Guadalupe. "She is the Mother of the Americas, and therefore the merciful mother of our continent and our country," Dr. Thatcher explained. "We want her to watch over our work with her maternal compassion, because so many people, even in affluent North America, are longing to experience her Son's mercy."

The Story of Mary's Appearances in Guadalupe

In fact, the Blessed Virgin of Guadalupe had a profound impact on the very earliest days of Christian evangelization in the Americas. In 1531, she appeared in Mexico on four occasions to a poor native Aztec named Juan Diego (canonized a saint in 2002). She asked him to bear a message to the local bishop that a new chapel should be built in her honor at Tepeyac Hill. Twice Juan went to the bishop, and both times the request was rejected. The bishop was not convinced that Our Lady had actually appeared to Juan Diego, and so he asked for a sign from Heaven to confirm Juan's story. Our Lady then told Juan to go a third time and said, "Come here [to Tepeyac Hill] tomorrow so that you may take the bishop the sign that he has asked for. Go now, I will be waiting for you tomorrow."

With his uncle sick and on the verge of death, Juan did not do as he was asked. On December 12, he took a different path from the one where he had originally seen Our Lady, hoping that he would not see her so that she would not delay his trip to the village for a priest. Nonetheless, she appeared to Juan on this new path, told him that his uncle was already well, and instructed him to climb to the top of Tepeyac Hill and gather the flowers he would find there in his cactus fiber cloak (called a "*tilma*"). Juan climbed to the usually barren top of the hill and, much to his surprise, found beautiful Castilian roses there in full bloom in winter, which he carefully gathered in the fold of his cloak to take to the bishop. When he reached the bishop's residence and opened the *tilma* to let the roses fall to the ground, however, the bishop and his aides were amazed to see a life-sized image of Our Lady imprinted on Juan Diego's *tilma*.

The first EADM *Cenacle Formation Manual* clearly explains some of the elaborate symbolism encoded in this miraculous image:

> The Image of Our Lady of Guadalupe reveals her clothed with the sun atop a crescent-shaped moon,

symbolizing her greatness — more than the sun or moon gods worshipped by the Aztecs at that time. She is wearing a turquoise blue mantle symbolic of royalty, and a rose-colored gown, symbolic of Divine Love. Her head is tilted down as a position of humility, symbolic of her being a servant of God. The black band around her waist and the four-leaf flower on her gown are symbolic of her being with Child. The small finger on her hand is separated from the others, indicating to the Indians that they must believe in the One True God and the Trinity.

Providentially, the image also portrays Mary as a "*mestiza*," a person of both Spanish and Indian blood. This clearly showed that she wanted to transcend the cultural divide between the native inhabitants of Mexico and the European colonists who had conquered, exploited, and mistreated them. All were to be united in devotion to her Son. Mary appeared, therefore, as a harbinger of peace and reconciliation.

This image of Our Lady had such a powerful impact upon the Aztec nation that in the five years after its appearance, approximately 8 million Aztecs and other local natives were converted to the Catholic Faith! The Blessed Virgin thereby helped conclusively put a stop to the most horrific aspect of Aztec culture: the barbaric practice of human sacrifice. For example, six years before Columbus arrived in the New World, a new temple was built in Mexico by the Aztecs. There were four days of ritual sacrifice to celebrate the occasion, during which 72,344 people were sacrificed to the Aztec gods by having their chests cut open and their hearts pulled out while they were still alive.

The conversion of the Aztecs to the Catholic faith, however, put an end to this terrible religious practice once and for all. Today, 15 million pilgrims a year come to Guadalupe to view the miraculous image of Our Lady, the Mother of the Americas — including St. Pope John Paul II in 1979, 1990, 1999, and 2002. Many pilgrims come to the Shrine to pray for an end to the human sacrifice of abortion and the anti-life mentality of our modern culture of death. As Mary appears in the image as a pregnant woman, carrying the Child Jesus within her, so she is the protectress of all innocent unborn life, and filled with compassion, too, for mothers who have to bring their children into the world in difficult circumstances, as Mary herself did when "she brought forth her first-born son, and wrapped him in swaddling clothes and laid him in a manger, because there was no room for them in the inn" (Lk 2:7).

The Image of Our Lady of Guadalupe Astounds Scientists

Of course, skeptics claim that the whole story of Guadalupe is nothing but legend and superstition. But try telling that to Professor Phillip Callahan of the University of Florida and Professor Jody Smith of Pensacola, who took some 60 photographs of the sacred image in 1979, many in infrared, to determine if there was a preliminary artist's drawing under the picture. Other photographs were computer-enhanced and studied for clues as to the image's origin. Francis Johnson reports their findings in his book *The Wonder of Guadalupe* (TAN Books, 1981):

> The picture dating from 1531 cannot be explained by science. Its colour rendering and the preservation of its brightness over the centuries are inexplicable. There is definitely no under-drawing, no sizing and no protective over-varnish present on the image. Without sizing, the "tilma" [made of cactus fibers, which typically disintegrate after only 20 years] should have rotted centuries ago, and without protective varnishing, the picture should have been ruined long ago by prolonged exposure to candle smoke and other pollutants ... Under high magnification, the image shows no detectable sign of fading or cracking — an inexplicable occurrence after 450 years of existence. Powerful lenses also revealed the astonishing fact that the coarse weave of the "tilma" had been deliberately utilized in a precise manner to give depth to the face of

the image ... The infra-red close-up pictures show no brush-marks, and the absence of sizing is patent in the many unfilled spaces visible in the fabric ...

The pink robe and especially the blue mantle of the Virgin merited closer study, since all the known pigments that could have been used to produce them would have faded long ago, and the torrid Mexican summers would only have accelerated this process. Yet the coloring remains as brilliant and as fresh as if it had just been laid on. The pink coloring of the robe was found to be transparent to infra-red light, and this highlighted another mystery. Most pink pigments are opaque to infra-red light, but there is no trace in the image of the few that are not.

"Studying the image," Professor Callahan concluded, "was the most moving experience of my life ... . It may seem strange for a scientist to say this, but as far as I am concerned, the original picture is miraculous."

The wonders of the Image of Our Lady of Guadalupe are truly astonishing. Father Peter John Cameron, OP, lists several more of them for us in his book *Mysteries of the Virgin Mary* (pp. 131-132):

Scientific research on the tilma reveals that microscopic images of Juan Diego, Bishop Zumarraga, and others are reflected in the eyes of our Lady. This suggests that she was an invisible presence in the room when Juan Diego presented the flowers: Mary chose to include a picture of herself as she stood watching the scene ... .

What is more, the tilma has proven to be indestructible. An accidental spill of nitric acid over the left side of the image in 1785 left the fabric undamaged. And a 1921 bomb placed at the foot of the image bent the heavy iron crucifix on the altar and blew out the windows of the neighbors but did no harm whatsoever to the image or to the glass shielding it ... .

The Message of Guadalupe for Today

EADM promotes the beauty and sanctity of life from conception to natural death. Their mission statement calls them to pray and work for an end to abortion, and to do acts of mercy with a focus on the "lepers" of today: the rejected, the lonely, the disabled, the elderly, and the dying. It is no wonder, therefore, that they have placed all their labors under the patronage of Our Lady of Guadalupe, the Blessed Virgin of the miraculous image, who put an end to the slaughter of innocents in the days of the Aztecs, and who upholds the dignity of all human life by her powerful intercessions today. She reassures us all with the maternal words she spoke to St. Juan Diego:

> Am I not here, I who am your mother? Are you not under my shadow and protection? Am I not the source of your joy? Are you not in the folds of my mantle, in the crossing of my arms? Is there anything else you need?"

The message of Guadalupe is also a message of reconciliation among people of different cultural and ethnic backgrounds. In a world in which racism never lurks far below the surface, the pregnant, royal *mestiza* of Guadalupe reminds us that she is the rightful mother and queen of the entire human race, and of all peoples (all who share the same moon and sun) — that we are all meant to be one family, and one spiritual race in Christ: "There is neither Jew nor Greek, there is neither slave nor free, there is neither male nor female, for you are all one in Christ Jesus" (Gal 3:28).

Moreover, the story of Guadalupe shows us that in Christ's mission to bring the graces of conversion to the Americas, the laity of the Church have a special role to play. Like St. Juan Diego, we may be people with no earthly status, no great wealth or education, and no ecclesiastical position. But Our Lady can use us in the service of her Son to work out His plan for the conversion of North, Central, and South America to the fullness of the Catholic Faith, and to help defeat the forces of evil that uphold the culture of death in our time: the culture of abortion and euthanasia, poverty and drug addiction, violent crime and suicide. Whether Our Lady calls us to play a public role as part of her triumph in the Americas, or merely asks us to serve, in hidden and quiet ways, the needs of the lost and the broken, the message of Guadalupe is that many of her special assistants will be Christ's faithful laity, prefigured in St. Juan Diego.

A PRAYER FOR REVERENCE FOR LIFE

Almighty God, we thank you for the precious gift of
   human life,
For life in the womb, coming from your creative power,
For the life of children, making us glad with their
   freshness and promise,
For the life of young people, hoping for a better world,
For the life of the disabled, teaching us that every life
   has value,
For the life of the elderly, witnessing to the ageless
   values of patience and wisdom.

Like Blessed Mary, may we always say "yes" to your gift,
May we defend it and promote it from conception to its
   natural end,
And bring us at last, O Father, to the fullness of eternal
   life,
Through Jesus Christ our Lord. Amen

QUESTIONS FOR DISCUSSION

1. What was happening to the Catholic Church in
   Europe at the same time that Our Lady appeared to
   St. Juan Diego (the 1530s), and what does this tell
   us about the faithfulness of our Lord to His Church,
   despite the sins and failings of many individual
   Catholics?

2. Was the bishop wrong to ask for a sign from Heaven that Juan Diego was telling the truth about the appearances of Our Lady and her request for a church to be built in her honor? How did Our Lady use this circumstance to work a miracle for her beloved Aztec people?

3. What do you see as the message of the story of Our Lady of Guadalupe to North Americans today?

2. OUR LADY OF LOURDES, FRANCE, 1858

Lourdes, France, is the most visited Marian pilgrimage site in the world, and attracts millions of Christians of many denominations each year. It's hard to believe, but back in 1858, the ancient rock promontory shooting skyward from the ground just past the River Gave was literally a dump, used by the townspeople as a place for trash.

The Story of Our Lady of Lourdes

The "Massabielle" ("Big Rock"), as the locals called it, was a dank, dark place, hardly fitting for the Mother of God. The jutting rock face has two geological quirks: a grotto 26 feet deep by 37 feet wide and, to the right of the grotto and above, a small niche. The grotto's unsightly appearance and desolation kept most people away, including Bernadette Soubirous, 14, a poor, sickly, uneducated peasant girl from Lourdes. Bernadette had heard of Massabielle but never went there. That changed on February 11, 1858, when she and two other girls — her sister Toinette and school chum Jeanne Abadie — went to the grotto looking for firewood.

The girls separated, and Bernadette was alone in the grotto. Taking off her shoes and socks, she tried to cross the shallow water of the river. She heard what sounded like a rush of wind, though the tree branches and bushes didn't move. After again hearing the sound, she looked at the grotto. To her astonishment, she testified, "I saw a lady dressed in white, wearing a white dress, a blue girdle, and a yellow rose on each foot, the same color as the chain of her rosary." Bernadette felt a "violent impression" until the Lady took her rosary beads and made the Sign of the Cross. After that, she said, "I commenced not to be afraid."

The Lady made a sign for Bernadette to approach, but the girl reported, "I stayed in the same place. Then, all of a sudden, she disappeared." When Bernadette caught up with her companions, she asked if they had seen anything unusual. They answered no. Bernadette thought she had been mistaken. Realizing she alone had seen the mysterious figure, Bernadette asked her sister not to say anything to their mother, but Toinette couldn't hold her tongue. Upon hearing the story, Bernadette's mother insisted that these were illusions, and told her daughter not to return to the grotto. But, driven by an interior impulse, Bernadette went back to Big Rock. There, on February 14, the "small, young lady reappeared," but again did not speak. On the third visit, Bernadette said that the "beautiful lady" asked that she return to the same site daily for 15 days. "I promise to make you happy not in this world but in the next," the Lady told Bernadette. On February 24, the Lady asked for prayer and penance for the conversion of sinners. On February 25, with word having gotten out about the strange occurrences at Massabielle, hundreds of people accompanied Bernadette to her appointment with the Lady. The people saw nothing other than Bernadette acting strangely. The Lady had told Bernadette to dig the ground and drink the water she found there. The people thought her mad. The police commissioner even barred her from entering the grounds. But still Bernadette came, and the crowds followed, including a woman named Catherine Latapie. With two fingers paralyzed from a fall she had taken two years prior, Catherine dipped her hands into the spring and her fingers were healed.

On March 2, more than 1,600 people accompanied Bernadette to Massabielle. Many of the people were already referring to the Lady as the "Blessed Virgin." In this apparition, the Lady asked that a chapel be built, and that people come in procession. The local priest, Abbe Peyramele, said the chapel could not be built until the Lady's name was known. It wasn't until the 16th apparition, on March 25, that the lady identified herself, stating, "I am the Immaculate Conception." Upon being notified of the Lady's words, the doubts of the local pastor, Abbe Peyramale, dissipated. After all, only four years prior, the Magisterium of the Church had proclaimed Mary's Immaculate Conception a dogma of the Church, something Bernadette had not yet heard of or known. Pope Pius IX, in 1854, had declared that Mary was, "from the first moment of her conception, by a singular grace and privilege of almighty God and by virtue of the merits of Jesus Christ, Savior of the human race, preserved immune from all stain of original sin." God preserved Mary from all stain of sin in light of the unique role she would play as mother of His Son (see Chapters Three and Five).

Bernadette went to the grotto for the last time on July 16, 1858. It was the 18th apparition. Mary didn't speak, but Bernadette knew it would be the last apparition. "I have never seen her so beautiful before," she said.

The Church opened an official investigation into the apparitions on November 17, 1858, and on January 18, 1860, the local bishop finally declared "the Virgin Mary did indeed appear to Bernadette Soubirous."

The Aftermath of the Apparitions

The spring in the grotto has been a focal point of all pilgrimages to Lourdes since the time of Bernadette, and a source of healing, too, both spiritual and physical. Since 1858, more than 7,000 people have come forward to report healings from the waters of Lourdes, hoping to have the Church proclaim a miracle. In conjunction with the Catholic Church, the Lourdes Medical Bureau examines all cases. Of the 7,000-plus, 67 are officially recognized as scientifically inexplicable (that is, miraculous). And the other cases are not declared to be definitely "non-miraculous": In most instances, there is just insufficient evidence to be sure one way or the other. The number of actual miraculous cures at Lourdes, therefore, could number well into the hundreds.

Several churches were eventually built at Lourdes, including the Basilica of St. Pius X. It is large enough that up to 25,000 people can attend Mass at a time. Many believe that Lourdes is the greatest Marian shrine of the Church, and several million pilgrims visit each year.

The events at Lourdes had an enormous impact, helping to strengthen the faith of Catholics during an era of revolution and revolt in Europe in which many were abandoning their faith. The Church celebrates a Mass in honor of "Our Lady of Lourdes" (optional memorial) in many countries on February 11 of each year — the anniversary of the first apparition.

In 1957, Pope Pius XII wrote an encyclical, *Le Pelerinage de Lourdes* (*The Pilgrimage to Lourdes*), on the apparitions. In this document, the Holy Father spoke of Mary as a mother with a tender and compassionate love for all people. He wrote:

> Go to her, you who are crushed by material misery, defenseless against the hardships of life and the indifference of men. Go to her, you who are assailed by sorrows and moral trials. Go to her, beloved invalids

and infirm, you who are sincerely welcomed and honored at Lourdes as the suffering members of our Lord. Go to her and receive peace of heart, strength for your daily duties, joy for the sacrifice you offer (57).

The Immaculate Virgin, who knows the secret ways by which grace operates in souls and the silent work of this supernatural leaven in this world, knows also the great price which God attaches to your sufferings united to those of the Savior. They can greatly contribute, we have no doubt, to this Christian renewal of society which we implore of God through the powerful intercession of His Mother (58).

Bernadette Soubirous eventually joined a convent and learned to read and write. At the age of 22, Bernadette became a Sister of Charity at Nevers, France. She sought God in the silence of the cloister, and she served Him there in humility. She also suffered for many years from tuberculosis of the bone, and died at the young age of 35. Bernadette spent a good portion of her last years in the infirmary. When a fellow nun accused her of being a "lazybones," Bernadette said, "My job is to be ill." She was canonized a saint on December 8, 1933, and her feast day is April 16. Her incorrupt body lies in a chapel in St. Gildard Convent in Nevers, France.

PRAYER

Oh ever immaculate Virgin, Mother of Mercy, Health of the Sick, Refuge of Sinners, Comforter of the Afflicted, you know my wants, my troubles, and my sufferings. Look upon me with mercy. When you appeared in the grotto of Lourdes, you made it a privileged sanctuary from which you dispense your favors and a place where many sufferers have obtained the cure of their infirmities, both spiritual and corporal. I come, therefore, with unbounded confidence to implore your maternal intercession. Through your loving compassion, shown to thousands of pilgrims who come to your shrine at Lourdes, and through your special love for your devoted child, Bernadette, I ask for this grace, if it be the Will of God: _____.

Our Lady of Lourdes, aid me through your prayers to your Divine Son to be a true child of yours, as Bernadette was, and to grow daily in your likeness.

My loving Mother, obtain my request. I will try to imitate your virtues so that I may one day share your company and bless you in eternity. Amen.

(Adapted from a prayer by Fr. Laurence Lovasik, SVD.)

QUESTIONS FOR DISCUSSION:

1. Why do you think the Blessed Mother appeared in Lourdes in 1858?

2. Discuss what the phrase "I am the Immaculate Conception" means (see *CCC*, 491-492).

3. In view of the grace received by Mary from God, does this apparition deepen your understanding of why the Church honors Mary?

3. OUR LADY OF FATIMA, PORTUGAL, 1917

When Our Lady first appeared to three shepherd children in Fatima, Portugal, on May 13, 1917, much of the world's social order was on the brink of collapse. The death toll mounted with brutal efficiency as World War I raged. In Russia, Lenin was just five months away from leading the Bolshevik Revolution, which ushered in the evils and dehumanization of Soviet Communism.

Over a six month period, from May 13 to October 13, 1917, Our Lady appeared to three children: Lucia dos Santos and her two cousins, Francisco and Jacinta Marto. She said Heaven would establish peace if people responded to her requests for prayer, reparation, and consecration.

Herding sheep at a location known as "Cova da Iria" ("Irene's Cove") near their home village of Fatima in Portugal on May 13, 1917, the three children suddenly heard lightning. Then, just above an oak tree, they saw a beautiful Lady holding a rosary in her hand. Lucia described the woman as "brighter than the sun, giving out rays of clear and intense light, just like a crystal goblet full of pure water when the fiery sun passes through it." Over the course of the 1917 apparitions, Mary identified herself as "Our Lady of the Rosary." She urged prayer and penance for the conversion of sinners and the papal consecration, in union with the bishops of the world, of Russia to her Immaculate Heart. Our Lady told the children that war was a consequence of sin and disobedience, and that God would permit the chastisement of the earth through war, hunger, and persecution of the Church, including the Holy Father and the faithful. Russia would be a tool of this chastisement, and would spread its errors around the globe. Further, Our Lady asked the children to do penance and to make sacrifices of reparation to save sinners. Lucia reported that the Blessed Mother urged the children to pray a Rosary daily.

On July 13, Our Lady promised there would be a miracle on her last visit in October so that all would believe. After a heavy rain lasting more than a day, a thin layer of clouds surrounded the sun on October 13, 2017. With more than 70,000 people in attendance, including news reporters and photographers, Lucia called out for the crowd to look at the sun. The sun appeared to change colors and rotate, and it seemed as if the sun was falling and going to crash into the earth. A writer for Portugal's influential newspaper *O Seculo* reported that, before the astonished eyes of the crowd, whose aspect was biblical as they stood bare-headed, eagerly searching the sky, the sun trembled and made sudden incredible movements outside all cosmic laws — indeed, the sun "danced," according to the typical expression of many people. However, not all saw the sun dance, and some in attendance claimed they saw nothing at all. While the crowd stared at the sun, the seers were staring at apparitions of the Child Jesus, the Blessed Virgin Mary (alternately adorned with the symbols of some of her various titles, such as Our Lady of Mount Carmel), and St. Joseph — that is, the Holy Family. There were other reports in the surrounding area of unusual activity of the sun. Some who saw the miracle were atheists or unbelievers at the time, and others who saw the miracle were as much as 40 miles away. These witnesses are solid evidence that this was not just a pious hallucination of the Catholic faithful assembled at the Cova that day.

The essence of the message from Our Lady in these apparitions is contained in what became known as the "secret of Fatima," which Our Lady delivered on July 13, 1917. First, she revealed to the children a vision of hell where the souls of poor sinners would go. The Blessed Mother asked for prayers and repentance to save such souls.

In her memoirs, Lucia wrote, "Our Lady showed us a great sea of fire which seemed to be under the earth. Plunged in this fire were demons and souls in human form, like transparent burning embers, all blackened or burnished bronze, floating about in the conflagration, now raised into the air by the flames ... How can we ever be grateful enough to our kind heavenly Mother, who had already prepared us by promising, in the first Apparition, to take us to heaven. Otherwise, I think we would have died of fear and terror." Lucia said that Our Lady encouraged acts of reparation and prayers to console Jesus for the sins of mankind. She also prophesied a second world war, and specifically asked for First Saturdays of Reparation and that Russia be consecrated to her Immaculate Heart. She predicted the forthcoming triumph of her Immaculate Heart, following Russia's consecration and conversion. Lucia, in her third memoir, wrote, "You have seen hell where the souls of poor sinners go. To save them, God wishes to establish in the world devotion to my Immaculate Heart. If what I say to you is done, many souls will be saved and there will be peace."

Several popes performed consecrations of the world to the Immaculate Heart (both Venerable Pope Pius XII and St. Pope John Paul II had a special devotion to Our Lady of Fatima), but the consecration that counted the most was done by St. John Paul II in 1984, a few short years after he was shot on May 13, 1981 before a general audience in St. Peter's Square. Our Lady of Fatima is credited by many — even by John Paul II himself — with saving the Holy Father's life during the assassination attempt. During his convalescence, he asked for the third secret of Fatima and the *Diary* of St. Faustina to be brought to his bedside (which, by the way, indicates that he discerned a connection between the Divine Mercy message and devotion given by Jesus through St. Faustina, and the Fatima message given by Our Lady through the three little visionaries). In light of Our Lady's miraculous intercession to preserve his life, St. John Paul II set out to make the requested consecration of Russia. In 1989, Sr. Lucia stated through the Carmelite nuns in Portugal that the collegial consecration of Russia to her Immaculate Heart that Our Lady had requested had been accomplished by Pope John Paul II on March 24, 1984. After that consecration, countries in Eastern Europe overcame Communist oppression, culminating in the fall of the Berlin Wall, the collapse of the Soviet Union, and the end of the Iron Curtain dividing Europe.

What is known as the "Third Secret" was contained in writings from Lucia that were withheld by the Holy See until May 13, 2000. There was an agreement with the bishop of Leiria, Portugal, whose diocese contains Fatima, not to release the secret before 1960 or only after Lucia's death. Many speculated that this portion of the secret concerned chaos in the Catholic Church, predicting widespread apostasy and a loss of faith beginning in the last half of the 20th century.

The following is what Sr. Lucia wrote about the third secret (or, really, the third part of the one secret of Fatima):

> I write in obedience to you, my God, who command me to do so through his Excellency the Bishop of Leiria and through your Most Holy Mother and mine.
>
> After the two parts which I have already explained, at the left of Our Lady and a little above, we saw an Angel with a flaming sword in his left hand; flashing, it gave out flames that looked as though they would set the world on fire; but they died out in contact with the splendour that Our Lady radiated towards him from her right hand: pointing to the earth with his right hand, the Angel cried out in a loud voice: 'Penance, Penance, Penance!'. And we saw in an immense light that is God: 'something similar to how people appear in a mirror when they pass in front of it' a Bishop dressed in White 'we had the impression that it was the Holy Father'. Other Bishops, Priests, men and women Religious going up a steep mountain, at the top of which there was a big Cross of rough-hewn trunks as of a cork-tree with the bark; before reaching there the Holy Father passed through a big city half in ruins and half trembling with halting step, afflicted with pain and sorrow, he prayed for the souls of the corpses he met on his way; having reached the top of the mountain, on his knees at the foot of the big Cross he was killed by a group of soldiers who fired bullets and arrows at him, and in the same way there died one after another the other Bishops, Priests, men and women Religious, and various lay people of different ranks and positions.

Beneath the two arms of the Cross there were two Angels each with a crystal aspersorium [liturgical implements for sprinkling holy water] in his hand, in which they gathered up the blood of the Martyrs and with it sprinkled the souls that were making their way to God.

Father Robert Fox, founder and director of the International Fatima Family Apostolate, wrote in the Fall 2000 issue of *Marian Helper* magazine that the Third Secret described in imagery the 1981 assassination attempt on the life of Pope John Paul II, as well as the persecution of many Christians who were martyred during the 20th century.

But Fatima's message to us has not been completely fulfilled or lost its relevance. On May 13, 2010, during a visit to the shrine at Fatima, Pope Benedict XVI said:

> We would be mistaken to think that Fatima's prophetic mission is complete. Here there takes on new life the plan of God which asks humanity from the beginning: "Where is your brother Abel […] Your brother's blood is crying out to me from the ground!" (Gen 4:9). Mankind has succeeded in unleashing a cycle of death and terror, but failed in bringing it to an end … In sacred Scripture we often find that God seeks righteous men and women in order to save the city of man and he does the same here, in Fatima, when Our Lady asks: "Do you want to offer yourselves to God, to endure all the sufferings which he will send you, in an act of reparation for the sins by which he is offended and of supplication for the conversion of sinners?" (*Memoirs of Sister Lúcia*, I, 162).

Fatima calls all of us to reparation and prayer, especially through the consecration of Russia, the world, and each of us individually to the Immaculate Heart of Mary, our mother.

What became of the visionaries? Lucia reportedly saw Our Lady in private apparitions throughout her life. She became a nun but left the Dorothean order in 1947 to join the Discalced Carmelite Order; she died at the age of 97 on February 13,

2005. Francisco and Jacinta died young, passing to their heavenly reward in the Great Flu Epidemic of 1918-20. Lucia stated that Our Lady had predicted their deaths at the second apparition in June 1917. Olimpia Marto, mother of the two younger visionaries, said that the children were aware of this and happily predicted their deaths to her and others on numerous occasions. Our Lady told Lucia she would remain on earth to help make Our Lady more known in this life. On May 13, 2000, during the Great Jubilee of the Incarnation, Francisco and Jacinta were declared "Blessed," a title of veneration just below sainthood. With Sr. Lucia present among the faithful at the shrine in Fatima, the beatification was carried out by St. John Paul II, the "bishop in white" who had been shot on that same date in 1981, the Feast of Our Lady of Fatima and the anniversary of the first Marian apparition at Fatima.

Today, there are year-round pilgrimages to Fatima. Additional chapels, hospitals, and other facilities have been built on the spectacular and holy grounds of the shrine. The largest crowds gather on May 13 and October 13, when up to a million pilgrims pray and observe the procession of a statue of Our Lady of Fatima (in whose crown is one of the bullets from the 1981 assassination attempt on St. John Paul II), and thousands participate in the candle processions on the grounds.

The message of Our Lady of Fatima remains a powerful one today, a message of hope. In a world in which the darkness of atheism, skepticism, and moral relativism seems to be spreading across the globe, and violence and terrorism are on the rise, she offers us hope that, in the end, her Immaculate Heart will triumph despite the sins and errors of humanity, and the world will finally enjoy a period of peace and spiritual renewal. Moreover, she points us above all to her Immaculate Heart as the vessel of grace for this triumph, a Heart (as we saw in Chapter Nine of this book) that overflows with merciful love for all of us, her children. There is nothing that humanity needs more today than to draw near to the Heart of Mary, and to find in the chapel of her Heart the merciful love of her Son, our Savior Jesus Christ.

So how do we draw near to the Immaculate Heart of this most loving of mothers? Devotees of Our Lady of Fatima (such as the members of the Marian Fathers' Thirteenth of the Month

Club) are mindful of her plea that all of the faithful try to say a Rosary, or at least part of a Rosary, each and every day, especially for peace in the world and the conversion of sinners. Among those devotees is Pope Francis, who was inspired by the example of St. John Paul II to pray a complete Rosary every day, and who asked the bishop of Leiria, Portugal, to consecrate his pontificate to Our Lady of Fatima, which the bishop did in 2013. Devotees of Our Lady of Fatima are also eager to go to Confession and receive Holy Communion, pray five decades of the Rosary, and meditate on the Mysteries of the Rosary for at least 15 minutes on five consecutive First Saturdays of the month, offering their Holy Communion in reparation to Mary's Immaculate Heart. Of course, those devoted to Our Lady of Fatima can and should continue to make the First Saturdays devotion repeatedly throughout their lifetime as an act of love and a great spiritual practice, offering Our Lady consolation in this age of unbelief and disrespect toward sacred people and things. Fatima devotees may want to make a total consecration to Jesus through Mary Immaculate, using a preparation for consecration such as *33 Days to Morning Glory* by Fr. Michael Gaitley, MIC. Most of all, they turn to Our Lady in hope, trusting in her intercession as the loving spiritual mother of all humanity, and eagerly await the promised triumph of her Immaculate Heart.

PRAYER

O Immaculate Heart of Mary, guide me in the battle for souls. Make me a true apostle of your Triumph. Place my heart among the ranks of your chosen cohort, in the service of your Son in a special way. Send me forth into the world that I might gain for you even a single heart to present to God our Father, as your donation of salvation. Join my consecrated heart with those you have chosen to lead this force of truth. Help me, dear Mother, not to waver even for a moment, but to stand strong, committed to your Triumph. Amen.

(Adapted from a prayer by Fr. Dominik Maria.)

QUESTIONS FOR DISCUSSION:

1. Describe the first part of the secret of Fatima and the Church's teaching on hell (see *Catechism*, 1033-1037).

2. Lucia was told that God wants devotion to Mary's Immaculate Heart. How can we strengthen this devotion in our own lives, and how is Mary's Heart united with the Heart of Jesus, the Divine Mercy?

3. What small daily acts of reparation can you do to console our Lord for the sins of the world?

4. OUR LADY OF KIBEHO, RWANDA, 1981

The remarkable apparitions of Our Lady at Kibeho are the first approved Marian apparitions to take place in sub-Saharan Africa. The many signs and wonders that accompanied them served to highlight the profound importance of the call of the Mother of the Word to meditate on her Seven Sorrows as a means of receiving the graces we need to repent of our sins, heal the hardness of our hearts, and reconcile with God and neighbor.

But first, most North American readers of this book will need some basic background information on Kibeho, Rwanda.

Rwanda is a small country located on the equator in East Central Africa. It is surrounded by Burundi, Tanzania, Uganda, and the Republic of the Congo. Slightly smaller than the state of Maryland and surrounded by steep mountains and deep valleys, some have given it the name "the Little Switzerland of Africa." The Virunga Mountains, which include the volcano Karisimbi, is the highest point at 14,187 feet above sea level. The capital and largest city is Kigali. Rwanda's estimated population in 2009 was over 10 million. The life expectancy of the people is slightly over 50 years of age.

The Twa, a pygmy people who now make up only 1 percent of the population, were the original inhabitants of Rwanda. While the Hutu and Tutsi tribes are often considered to be two

separate ethnic groups, they have a history of intermarriage, speak the same language, and have many similar cultural characteristics. The main difference between the groups is that the Hutu are typically more involved in farming, while the Tutsi are cattle owners and ranchers. After World War I, Rwanda became a League of Nations mandate with Burundi, under the name of Rwanda-Burundi. The Belgian colonizers at first maintained Tutsi dominance, but over the years encouraged power-sharing between Hutu and Tutsi. Rwanda gained its full independence from colonial rule in 1962.

It was against this backdrop that the Blessed Mother appeared to several children in Rwanda in 1981. Six teenage girls and one boy claimed to see Our Lady and Jesus, but Bishop Misago of Gikongoro has approved only the visions of the first three: Alphonsine Mumureke, Anathalie Mukamazimpaka, and

Marie Claire Mukangango. Our Lady appeared to them under the title "Nyina wa Jambo," which means "Mother of the Word," synonymous to "Umubyeyl W'iamna" or "Mother of God."

Alphonsine was the first visionary, and on November 28, 1981, heard a voice calling her, saying, "My daughter." She asked, "Who are you?" The reply was "Ndi Nyina Wa Jambo," that is, "I am the Mother of the Word." The voice added, "I have come to calm you because I have heard your prayers. I would like your friends to have faith, because they do not believe strongly enough." Three and five months later, Our Lady began appearing to Anathalie and then Marie Claire respectively. The latter became a victim of the Rwandan genocide in 1994.

Our Lady stated:

> Although I am the Mother of God, I am simple and humble. I always place myself where you are. I love you as you are. I never reproach my little ones. When a child is without reproach in front of her mother, she will tell her everything that is in her heart. I am grateful when a child of mine is joyful with me. That joy is a most beautiful sign of trust and love. Few understand the mysteries of God's love. Let me as your mother embrace all my children with love so that you can confide your deepest longings to me. Know that I give all your longings to my Son Jesus, your brother.
>
> Nothing is more beautiful than a heart which offers its suffering to God. Pray, pray, pray. Follow the Gospel of my Son. Do not forget that God is more powerful than all the evil in the world. Share. Do not kill. Do not persecute. Respect the rights of man because if you act contrary to those rights, you will not succeed and it will come back against you.

During the apparitions in Kibeho, the Holy Virgin revealed that this Rosary of the Seven Sorrows possesses immense spiritual power for those who pray it with a sincere heart. Visionary Marie Clare explained, "We must meditate on the Passion of Jesus and on the deep sorrow of His Mother. We must recite the rosary and the beads of the Seven Sorrows of Our Lady to obtain the grace of repentance." When prayed with an open and repentant heart, this Rosary will obtain for us a deeper and more authentic contrition, infused with divine love, that prepares us for the Sacrament of Reconciliation and the forgiveness of our sins, freeing our souls from guilt and remorse. She also promised that, over time, this Rosary would develop within us a deep understanding of why we sin, knowledge which would give us the wisdom and strength to change or remove any internal faults, weaknesses of character, or personality flaws that cause us unhappiness and keep us from enjoying the joyful life God intended for us to have.

Devotion to the Seven Sorrows of Mary goes back to the Middle Ages, and the Seven Sorrows Rosary has long been promoted by the Servite Order. It includes 49 Hail Marys divided into groups of seven; each group of seven begins with an Our Father. The Seven Sorrows include:

The Presentation
The Flight into Egypt
The Loss of Jesus in Jerusalem
Mary Meeting Jesus on the Road to Calvary
Mary At the Foot of the Cross
Mary Receiving Jesus' Body
Jesus Laid in the Tomb

Alphonsine described Our Lady as she appeared at Kibeho, saying, "She had a seamless white dress and also a white veil on her head. Her hands were clasped together on her breast, and her fingers pointed to the sky ... I could not determine the color of her skin, but she was of incomparable beauty."

The content of the visions was generally joyful until August 19, 1982, when all the visionaries reported that the Virgin Mary asked everyone to pray to prevent a terrible war. They all reported seeing violence, dismembered corpses, and widespread destruction.

The fulfilment of this grim prophecy was not long in coming. It arrived in the form of a genocidal mass slaughter of Tutsi in Rwanda by members of the Hutu majority government. An estimated 800,000–1,000,000 Rwandans were killed during a 100-day period from April 7 to mid-July 1994, including as many as 70 percent of the Tutsi, 20 percent of Rwanda's total population — and dozens of children at the school in Kibeho, hacked to death by machetes. Overall, an estimated 2,000,000 Rwandans were displaced and became refugees. The genocide was deliberately planned by members of the core political elite, many of whom occupied positions at top levels of the national government.

In 2001, on the Solemnity of Sts. Peter and Paul, during a solemn Mass celebrated in the cathedral of Gikongoro, Bishop Augustin Misago declared the apparitions to be authentic, in part because of the terrible fulfilment of Our Lady's prophecy.

What do we need to take away from the apparitions of Our Lady of Kibeho? One of the most important truths made plain by these apparitions is the way in which our personal or private sins have dramatic public consequences. Our Lady asked for repentance, giving her children a devotion with unique power to help them do just that, to turn away from their sins and become transparent to the love of God, light to the nations, salt of the earth, and a city set on a hill. But, as genocide survivor Immaculee Ilibagiza has explained in her books, too many Rwandans did not listen, and so brother turned on brother, and the slaughter took place.

But Our Lady of Kibeho came to send a message to the world, not just to Rwandans. She came to remind us of a reality that's too easily forgotten in our industrial society, focused only on massive scale and efficient production: The true answer to global problems begins on the local, individual level, not on a gigantic scale. As she makes plain in her *Magnificat*, the Lord loves the lowly and lifts up the little ones of the world to the heights of true power and influence, of love and humility. Our Lady's answer to societal ills begins with personal, individual conversion, and she has come to give us the means to achieve it. We can become saints by God's grace, mediated to us through the Church, her Sacraments, and her members. We can become holy, people who live lives of love, conforming our minds to the truth, and thereby transform the world.

PRAYER

Prayer to Our Lady of Kibeho

Blessed Virgin Mary, Mother of the Word,
Mother of all those who believe in Him
and who welcome Him into their life,
we are here before you to contemplate You.
We believe that you are amongst us,
like a mother in the midst of her children,
even though we do not see You with our bodily eyes.

We bless You, the Sure Way that leads us to Jesus
    the Saviour,
for all the favours which You endlessly pour out upon us,
especially that, in your meekness, You were gracious
enough to appear miraculously in Kibeho,
just when our world needed it most.

Grant us always the light and the strength necessary
    to accept,
with all seriousness, Your call to us to be converted,
to repent, and to live according to your Son's Gospel.
Teach us how to pray with sincerity,
and to love one another as He loved us,
so that, just as You have requested,
we may always be beautiful flowers
diffusing their pleasant fragrance everywhere
and upon everyone.

Holy Mary, Our Lady of Sorrows,
teach us to understand the value of the cross in our lives,
so that whatever is still lacking to the sufferings of Christ
we may fill up in our own bodies for His mystical Body,
which is the Church.

And, when our pilgrimage on this earth comes to an end, may we live eternally with You in the kingdom of Heaven. Amen.

QUESTIONS FOR DISCUSSION:

1. Why did the Blessed Mother appear in Rwanda, and are the messages given to the children relevant for us today?

2. Discuss how the Blessed Mother responded to her Seven Sorrows, and the significance of this for your own life.

3. Discuss the relationship of Divine Mercy to the Rwandan genocide, and the role of forgiveness for all people, especially in our own lives.

SUGGESTIONS FOR FURTHER READING:

- Carl Anderson & Msgr. Edwardo Chavez, *Our Lady of Guadalupe: Mother of the Civilization of Love* (New York: Doubleday, 2009)

- Catherine Odell, *Those Who Saw Her* (Huntingdon, IN: Our Sunday Visitor, 2010)

- Father Michael Gaitley, MIC, *The Second Greatest Story Ever Told* (Marian Press, 2015)

- Father Donald Calloway, MIC, *Champions of the Rosary: The History and Heroes of a Spiritual Weapon* (Marian Press, 2016)

- Immaculée Ilibagiza, *Our Lady of Kibeho: Mary Speaks to the World From the Heart of Africa* (New York City: Hay House, Inc., 2008)

POSTSCRIPT:
Where Do We Go From Here?

If you have journeyed in this book through all of the central Catholic doctrines about Mary and some of her many appearances to the People of God, then the next question is unavoidable: "What do I do now? Where do I go from here?"

Remember that Mary's role in God's plan of salvation is to bring all of us closer to the Heart of Jesus, so ask her right now, in prayer, what she wants you to do. For example, if you are a member of EADM, you (or your EADM Cenacle) might consider consecrating yourselves to the Heart of Mary in a deeper way by following the do-it-yourself retreat manual *33 Days to Morning Glory* by Fr. Michael Gaitley, MIC (Marian Press, 2011). This best-selling book makes the whole Catholic tradition of consecration to Mary more practical and comprehensible than ever before. Also, Fr. Michael's *The Second Greatest Story Ever Told* (Marian Press, 2015) shares the role of Our Lady in the life and ministry of St. John Paul II, the significance and timeliness of her apparitions at Fatima, and more. Another excellent book to read would be Fr. Donald Calloway, MIC's personal testimony and in-depth teaching, *Under the Mantle: Marian Thoughts from a 21ˢᵗ Century Priest* (Marian Press, 2013), as well as his *Champions of the Rosary: The History and Heroes of a Spiritual Weapon* (Marian Press, 2016), a great overview of the history of the Rosary and the people who have prayed it, preserved it, and promoted it.

Other possibilities might include joining one of the Marian groups specifically centered on fostering devotion to Mary. For example, prayerfully consider whether you might be called to become a member of the Confraternity of the Immaculate Conception and/or be invested in the Blue Scapular. This confraternity involves a way of life and prayer that focuses especially on the imitation of Mary's 10 evangelical virtues. Or you might consider joining the Thirteenth of the Month Club, founded to help support vocations to the Marian Fathers of the Immaculate Conception and to pray the Rosary regularly. Named in honor of Our Lady's appearances in Fatima, the club has a monthly newsletter with articles related to devotion to Our Lady and the work of her devotees in the world today. Information about the confraternity and the club can be found at the website of the Marian Fathers: marian.org.

Finally, ask Our Lady how you can become a channel of Christ's merciful love to all those around you: your family, your friends, and your community. She will not fail to hear your prayer and answer you. By her example of trustful surrender, and by her prayers, she will always light the way!

Robert Stackpole, STD
Director, John Paul II Institute of Divine Mercy

ACKNOWLEDGMENTS

The author would like to thank Dr. Bryan Thatcher, MD, founder of the Eucharistic Apostles of The Divine Mercy, and Mr. Chris Sparks, MA, books editor for Marian Press, for their friendship, their encouragement with this project, and for all the extra help they provided for the chapter on the apparitions of Our Lady.

ENDNOTES

1 Fulton Sheen, *The World's First Love* (San Francisco: Ignatius Press, 2010), pp. 76-77. www.ignatius.com. Used with permission.

2 Mark Miravalle, *Introduction to Mary* (Goleta, CA: Queenship, 2006), pp. 214-215.

3 Scott Hahn, *Hail, Holy Queen* (New York: Image Books, 2001), pp. 27-28.

4 The Anglican-Roman Catholic International Commission Agreed Statement, *Mary: Grace and Hope in Christ* (Toronto: Novalis, 2005), p. x.

5 St. Bernard of Clairvaux, *In Praise of the Blessed Virgin Mary*, 4:8; cited in M. Basil Pennington, ed., *Bernard of Clairvaux: A Lover Teaching the Way of Love* (Hyde Park, NY: New City Press, 1997), pp. 27-29.

6 Miravalle, *Introduction to Mary*, pp. 52-53.

7 Ibid., p. 55.

8 John Henry Newman, *The Mystical Rose* (Princeton: Scepter, 1996), pp. 98 and 25-27.

9 Ibid., pp. 93-95 and 104; italics added.

10 Cited in Father Mateo, *Refuting the Attack on Mary* (El Cajon, CA: Catholic Answers, 1999), pp. 74-75.

11 It took several centuries for the early Christian writers to come to a consensus about the entire holiness of Mary. Some, such as St. Irenaeus in the second century, accused her of "excessive haste" at Cana, "seeking to push her son into performing a miracle before his hour had come" (*Adv. Haer.* II. 16.7). In the same era, Origen of Alexandria writes of her wavering in faith at the foot of the Cross, "so she too would have some sin for which Christ died" (*Hom.* in Lc. 17:6). Similar sentiments can be found in the fourth century in St. Basil of Caesarea, St. Hilary of Poitiers, and in the fifth by St. Cyril of Alexandria. In this book, however, we endeavor to show that the biblical stories of Mary in Cana and at the foot of the Cross do not support such skepticism. Already in the fourth century, St. Ephrem the Syrian was clearly arguing for the complete sanctity of Mary, and we find the same view supported early in the fifth century by St. Augustine, at least with regard to Mary's freedom from actual sin (*De natura et gratia* 36.42), and by Theodotus of Ancyra (*Homily* 6, 11). See ARCIC Agreed Statement, *Mary: Grace and Hope in Christ*, section 38, pp. 35-36. In short, here was a matter on which the ancient Fathers of the Church arrived at no consensus among themselves; it took several centuries for the saints, pondering these mysteries, to arrive at a consensus on the truth about the entire sanctity of Our Lady, just as Blessed John Henry Newman did.

12 For those inclined to be skeptical, the Anglican-Roman Catholic International Commission (ARCIC) provided an excellent summary of the historical evidence for the reliability of the virginal conception story in the Gospels:

> Given its strongly Jewish matrix in both Matthean and Lucan versions, an appeal to analogies with pagan mythology or to an exaltation of virginity over the married state to explain the origin of the tradition is implausible. Nor is the idea of virginal conception likely to derive from an over-literal reading of the Greek text

of Isaiah 7:14 ... for that is not the way the idea is introduced in the Lucan account [since Luke does not claim that the virginal conception fulfills any Old Testament prophecy]. Moreover, the suggestion that it originated as an answer to the accusation of illegitimacy levelled at Jesus is unlikely, as that accusation could equally have arisen because it was known that there was something unusual about Jesus' birth (Mk 6:3; Jn 8:41) and because of the Church's claim about his virginal conception. (ARCIC, *Mary, Grace and Hope in Christ*, section 18, pp. 18-19)

In short, while historical evidence all by itself cannot "prove" that Mary was a virgin when she conceived the Child Jesus in her womb, plausible alternative explanations are conspicuous by their absence!

[13] John Saward, *The Cradle of Redeeming Love* (San Francisco: Ignatius Press, 2002), pp. 212-213. www.ignatius.com. Used with permission.

[14] Hahn, *Hail, Holy Queen*, pp. 106-107.

[15] W.E. Vine, *An Expository Dictionary of New Testament Words* (Old Tappan, NJ: Fleming H. Revell, 1940), pp. 154-155.

[16] Tim Staples, *Behold Your Mother* (El Cajon: Catholic Answers Press, 2014), pp. 176-177.

[17] David Armstrong, *A Biblical Defense of Catholicism* (First Books edition, no date given), pp. 141-142.

[18] *Ignatius Catholic Study Bible: New Testament* (San Francisco: Ignatius Press, 2010), p. 8. www.ignatius.com. Used with permission.

[19] Miravalle, *Introduction to Mary*, pp. 222-223.

[20] Roch Kereszty, *Jesus Christ: Fundamentals of Christology* (New York: Society of St. Paul, 2002), p. 80.

[21] St. Jerome, *Against the Pelagians*, 2:4.

[22] Staples, *Behold Your Mother*, p. 158.

[23] St. Jerome, *On the Perpetual Virginity of Blessed Mary Against Helvidius*, 7.

[24] Adolf Faroni, *Know and Defend What You Love* (The Philippines: Don Bosco Press, no date given), p. 47.

[25] Newman, *Mystical Rose*, p. 13.

[26] St. John Chrysostom, *Epistle to the Ephesians* 1,1,3

[27] In *There is No Rose: the Mariology of the Catholic Church* (Minneapolis: Fortress Press, 2015), p. 9, Fr. Aidan Nichols, OP, makes the case that the most accurate translation would be "You who have already been transformed by grace."

[28] Newman, *Mystical Rose*, pp. 10-11.

[29] Cited in Miravalle, *Introduction to Mary*, p. 67.

[30] Cited in Staples, *Behold Your Mother*, pp. 64-65.

[31] The ancient Fathers of the Church were not unanimous in their understanding of when and how the Blessed Virgin was prepared by grace for her role as Mother of God. That is why it took the Church many centuries to ponder this mystery in greater depth. In the third century, for example, St. Gregory of Nazianzen seemed to teach that Mary was "pre-purified" at the moment of the Annunciation, and in the seventh century, St. Andrew of Crete taught that Mary was sanctified at the moment of her birth. In the eighth century, on the other hand, St. John Damascene taught that she was sanctified from the moment of conception — and that even the conjugal act of her parents that conceived her was specially graced by the Holy Spirit. Perhaps St. Augustine expressed the most common opinion when he conceded in his treatise *On*

Nature and Grace that all humanity was tainted by sin "except for the holy virgin Mary, about whom I do not wish any question to be raised when sin is being discussed — for whence do we know what greater grace or complete triumph over sin may have been given to her who merited to conceive and bear him who certainly was without sin." St. Augustine, *On Nature and Grace*, 36.42, cited in Nichols, *There is No Rose*, p. 51.

[32] Nicholas Cabasilas, *Homily on the Nativity of Mary*, 11, cited in Nichols, *There is No Rose*, p. 161.

[33] Louis Cameli, *Mary's Journey* (Notre Dame: Christian Classics, 2003), pp. 98 and 132.

[34] Fr. Peter John Cameron, OP, *Mysteries of the Virgin Mary* (Cincinnati: Servant Books, 2010), p. 87.

[35] Karl Keating, *Catholicism and Fundamentalism* (San Francisco: Ignatius Press, 1988), p. 274. www.ignatius.com. Used with permission. In fact, the only Marian relics known to the early Fathers of the Church were her robe and her girdle; Nichols, *There is No Rose*, p. 109.

[36] Cited in Staples, *Behold Your Mother*, p. 226

[37] St. Epiphanius, *Panarion*, 79,5,1

[38] Ibid., 78,23,8

[39] Hahn, *Hail, Holy Queen*, pp. 63-64.

[40] *Ignatius Catholic Study Bible: New Testament*, p. 107.

[41] Edward Sri, *Walking with Mary* (New York: Image Books, 2013), p. 161.

[42] See Hahn, *Hail, Holy Queen*, pp. 65-66, and ARCIC, *Mary, Grace and Hope in Christ*, section 29, p. 28.

[43] Edward Sri, "Decoding the Woman of the Apocalypse," in *Lay Witness*, March-April 2008, p. 11.

[44] Staples, *Behold Your Mother*, p. 212.

[45] Miravalle, *Introduction to Mary*, p. 74.

[46] NB: Here we deliberately refrain from pursuing this argument in the form often found in Catholic apologetics for both the Immaculate Conception and the Assumption. The argument goes like this: "The Son of God *ought* to have done these things for His Mother; He had the ability to do them; therefore He *must have* done them." While this can be a way of viewing these doctrines from the analogy of faith (i.e., it was certainly fitting that Christ did these things for His Mother), the argument is not logically compelling. As the prophet Isaiah has said, the Lord's thoughts are not our thoughts, nor His ways our ways (Is 55:8-9). He alone is all-knowing and infinitely wise. We do not have the kind of perspective on all things that would enable us to say what the Lord "ought to do" and "must have done" to express His love for His own earthly Mother.

[47] Mark Miravalle, *Mary: Co-Redemptrix, Advocate, Mediatrix of All Graces*, booklet, (Santa Barbara: Queenship Press, 1993), pp. 58-59.

[48] Miravalle, *Introduction to Mary*, pp. 41-42

[49] Cited in Orozco, *Mother of God and our Mother* (Princeton: Scepter, 1996) p. 65.

[50] Pope John Paul II, *Theotokos: Woman, Mother and Disciple* (Boston: Pauline Books and Media, 2000), p. 242.

[51] Staples, *Behold Your Mother*, pp. 283-284.

[52] *Introduction to Mary*, p. 105

[53] Hahn, *Hail, Holy Queen*, pp. 15-16.

[54] Bryan and Susan Thatcher, *Cenacle Formation Manual: Eucharistic Apostles of The Divine Mercy* (Stockbridge: Marian Press, 2002), pp. 74-75.

[55] Cameron, *Mysteries of the Virgin Mary*, p. 57.

[56] Staples, *Behold Your Mother*, p.229.

[57] Kenneth Howell, *Mary of Nazareth* (Santa Barbara, CA: Queenship Press, 1998), p. 31.

[58] Pope John Paul II, *Theotokos*, p. 189.

[59] Ibid., p. 190.

[60] Mark Miravalle, *Meet Your Mother* (Stockbridge; Marian Press, 2014), p. 8.

[61] Robert Stackpole, *Jesus, Mercy Incarnate* (Stockbridge: Marian Press, 2000), pp. 110-111.

[62] Saint John Eudes, *The Admirable Heart of Mary* (Buffalo, NY: Immaculate Heart Publications, reprint of 1947 edition), p. 14.

[63] Ibid., p. 20.

[64] Father Robert J. Fox, *True Devotion to the Immaculate Heart of Mary* (Fatima Family Apostolate International, 2005), pp. 84, 90, 92-96.

[65] Eudes, *The Admirable of Heart of Mary*, pp. 126-127.

[66] Mark Miravalle, "Mary: Mediatrix of Mercy" in *Divine Mercy: The Heart of the Gospel* (Stockbridge: The John Paul II Institute of Divine Mercy, 1999), p. 166.

[67] Fr. Michael Gaitley, MIC, *33 Days to Morning Glory* (Stockbridge: Marian Press, 2011), pp. 191-192. Father Gaitley is referring here to the belief that Mary acted on Calvary as a unique participant in her Son's saving Passion and Death. The idea was first developed in the work of theologians in the early Middle Ages, especially Paschasius Radbert, Arnold of Bonneval (friend and biographer of St. Bernard of Clairvaux), and in the *Mariale* of Pseudo-St. Albert. A common way of expressing the doctrine was that Mary suffered a compassion for the death of her Son so intense that it amounted to a *transfixio* of her Heart, a "spiritual crucifixion." This phrase and others similar to it were picked up and used later by many spiritual writers, saints, and popes, including St. John Paul II; see Nichols, *There is No Rose*, pp. 74-80.

INDEX

P

pagan 97-99, 169

Passion 24, 34, 84, 159, 172

Paul, St. 29, 35, 45, 52, 59, 62, 66, 68, 73-74, 83, 85, 92, 96, 128, 170

Peter, St. 74, 85, 92-93

Peter Chrysologus, St. 21

Protestant 9, 34, 36, 41, 46, 51-52, 63, 65-66, 73, 77, 82, 87, 95, 97, 108, 130

Protoevangelium 61

Q

Queen 3, 13, 15, 21, 57, 77, 87, 89, 91-95, 97, 99-100, 103, 107, 122-123, 133, 142, 169, 170-172

R

Rosary 145, 150-151, 156, 159-160, 163, 165-166

Russia 149-150, 152, 154

Russian Orthodox 65

S

Satan 61, 80, 83, 109, 112

Scripture 11, 14-15, 19, 26, 29, 34, 35, 37, 45-48, 52-54, 57, 60-61, 74-77, 79, 83-84, 93, 95, 97-98, 100, 107, 127, 154

Serbian Orthodox 65

Sophronius of Jerusalem, St. 37

Spouse of the Holy Spirit 5, 53-54

Staples, Tim 46-47, 53, 82, 99, 107, 170-172

statues 10-12, 155

St. Therese Institute of Faith and Mission 85

symbol/symbolic 11, 51, 80-82, 91-92, 109-110, 117, 138-139, 151

T

Temple 9, 11, 25, 35-36, 45, 51, 53, 78-79, 86, 103, 122-123, 139

Teresa of Calcutta, St. 124, 127, 133

Tertullian of Carthage 20

Thatcher, Dr. Bryan 137, 167

Theotokos 31-32, 171-172

Thrall, Margaret 36

Tradition 15, 41, 47-48, 50, 52, 54, 60, 65-66, 75, 83-84, 93, 117, 124, 127, 165, 169

Trinity 30, 54, 70, 87, 123, 139

Devotion to Mary

Mary 101 Kit includes:

- Mary 101 DVD • Mary book
- Rosary booklet • Mary Tri-fold card
- Pamphlets and prayercards
- and the products included in the 100th Anniversary of Fatima Pack (below).

100th Anniversary of Fatima Pack includes:

Y58-FAMPK

- 100th Anniversary of Fatima Guidebook
- Pamphlets and a prayercard
- 5" x 7" Our Lady of Fatima print (exclusive to the pack)

Y58-MKIT   Items also sold separately.

Champions of the Rosary:
The History and Heroes of a Spiritual Weapon

Champions of the Rosary, the latest book by bestselling author Fr. Donald Calloway, MIC, tells the powerful story of the history of the Rosary and the champions of this devotion. The Rosary is a spiritual sword with the power to conquer sin, defeat evil, and bring about peace. Read this book to deepen your understanding and love for praying the Rosary. Endorsed by 30 bishops from around the world!
Y58-CRBK

33 Days to Morning Glory

Begin an extraordinary 33-day journey to Marian consecration with four spiritual giants: St. Louis de Montfort, St. Maximilian Kolbe, St. Mother Teresa, and St. John Paul II. (208 pages.)

Y58-33DAY   *ebook*: Y58-EB33DAY
Also available as a group retreat!

For our complete line of books, prayercards, pamphlets, and more, visit ShopMercy.org or call 1-800-462-7426.